CHICAGO IN THE FIFTIES

REMEMBERING LIFE IN THE LOOP AND THE NEIGHBORHOODS

NEAL SAMORS AND MICHAEL WILLIAMS

CHICAGO IN THE FIFTIES

REMEMBERING LIFE IN THE LOOP AND THE NEIGHBORHOODS

CONTENTS

The Palmolive Building, c.1955

FOREWORD HUGH HEFNER

The city that I knew when I was growing up was on Chicago's extreme west side in the Montclare neighborhood, during a transitional time frame when milk and ice wagons could still be found drawn by horses. It seemed almost semi-rural back then. But there was also the magic of downtown Chicago, with that Lindbergh Beacon sweeping across the skies from the top of the Palmolive Building. That beacon represented the unknown, and the possibilities of life.

Our first Playboy office was not far from that building, at 11 E. Superior. We used to eat dinner regularly at a restaurant called Charmets on the corner of Chicago and Michigan Avenue. The Water Tower was right there and so was a clear view of the Palmolive Building, which, at that time, had no tall buildings in between. I remember standing on that corner and looking at the building, not realizing that within a few years we would own it.

During the 1950s, Chicago continued to be the center of the country. You couldn't go cross country by train in those years without going through Chicago — you had to change trains there. Because of this, many entertainers and celebrities were in the city, either performing or on the way from one coast to the other. When they did come through town, they would invariably come to the Playboy offices, the club or the "Playboy at Night" television show.

They call Chicago the "second city," but I was always sensitive to that perception, and was very much aware that both coasts were places that we could have relocated our base. It was during these years that many television and radio shows originally based in Chicago were taken away to New York City and Los Angeles. The same thing was true for a number of magazines that had started in Chicago and then pulled away.

I think that one of the things that helped Playboy is that Chicago, unlike New York and Los Angeles, is a truly American city, and it clearly reflects America. I think that both New York and Los Angeles are unique unto themselves, with personalities that make them almost independent countries, whereas Chicago is truly an American city.

Looking back, the greatest connection for me to the city is the Chicago of my childhood. The memories of that particular time and place were keys to me. Throughout the 1960s, Chicago for me was mostly my life at the mansion and the world I created. But the Chicago that I really love is the Chicago that influenced me when I was growing up and when I was a young adult, at the very beginning of the magazine.

In other words, it was in the 1950s that I came into my own, and really began to play out the dreams and fantasies that had grown and were nurtured in the Chicago of my youth. It was a very romantic period, and I would not have wanted to grow up any place other than Chicago.

Hugh Hefner attended Steinmetz High School and the University of Illinois before creating Playboy, *one of the most successful magazines of the twentieth century.*

Louis Armstrong at the Sutherland Hotel, c.1959
Photograph by John Puslis *Chicago Sun-Times*

BRONZEVILLE MEMORIES WARNER SAUNDERS

I was born in Chicago in 1935. My father was a Pullman porter and my mother was a maid, and we lived over a grocery store near 47th and South Parkway. That intersection might have been the most popular spot in Chicago at the time. In the book "Black Metropolis," the authors wrote that if any black person coming from the south would stand on the corner of 47th and South Parkway long enough during a Saturday afternoon, he would surely find someone from his or her hometown. Many blacks took the Illinois Central Railroad up from the south and got off at the 12th Street Station, as my mother did in 1923, and moved to the South Side — in what was considered the Black Belt — an amazing place to grow-up. Living there was unusual because of segregation — people of almost every ilk lived in that same community. So, you didn't see just one class of people. Instead, you saw the "best" and the "worst" all in one neighborhood.

It was exciting living near 47th Street because the Regal Theater and the Savoy Ballroom were right around the corner — the alley with the back door to the Regal literally faced our house. You talk about people watching! There were about ten children who lived in our apartment building, and we were all about the same age. We used to stand outside and, literally, watch the stars go by, and they included nearly every entertainer, athlete, and businessperson — there's Joe Louis, there's Count Basie, there's Ella Fitzgerald and there's Billy Eckstine. A lot of black entertainers lived in Chicago at that time, like Nat King Cole and Louis Armstrong. In fact, Louis lived right across the street from the Regal Theater. It was like State and Madison for the black community, and it was the center of everything. There was a large department store across the street called the South Center Department Store, and it was very much like a mini-Marshall Field's. So, they drew a lot of people, and, of course, the Regal and the Savoy Ballroom drew a lot of people. There were lines going around the corner waiting for those stage shows. So, we used to go and hang out on 47th Street and just watch — we didn't have to go far for our entertainment. Unfortunately, I never thought to get an autograph from anybody. You would see stars so often that you didn't bother to, because you would always expect to see them again.

It was a vibrant community, and it was exciting to live in such close proximity to all of these things that were going on. For instance, my father was a great boxing fan, and the nearby Savoy Ballroom was a great venue for amateur boxing. It was called "Tuesday Night Fights," and every Tuesday night we would go to the fights and I would sit ringside with my mother and father — that was our night out. Then, when I got old enough, I'd go to the Savoy for dances and roller skating — that was a big thing, too. There were many fun things to do on the South Side — like a place called White City. Although the original amusement park had already burned down, there still was one building operating there. I also had a strong interest in jazz when I was growing up, and there was a place called Warwick Hall on 47th Street where all of the wilder kids hung out. I used to love to go there and act bad! I wasn't old enough to go to the Club DeLisa yet, and by the time I was, it wasn't a hip place for us anymore.

Now, we were the first family in our building to get a television set, so we were the most popular family there! Everybody would come to our apartment to see the television — it was a little Halicrafter's set with a small, square screen. Of course, you put a big magnifier in front of it to make the picture larger in those days! My grandmother loved to watch the wrestling matches on Friday nights, and later on in the 1950s we would watch "Kukla, Fran and Ollie" and the "Milton Berle Show." One program that really touched us was Nat King Cole's 15-minute program. After he came on television, I remember the *Chicago Defender* had big headlines saying they wouldn't allow his program in the South because they didn't want him singing with white singers, particularly women singers.

Race was an issue in those years, and we had to be careful where we went. I used to love to go to the Museum of Science and Industry, the Field Museum and the Shedd Aquarium, and they were relatively less hostile to blacks than other places. I was also interested in art, and got a small scholarship to the Art Institute, where I used to draw and paint on the weekends. The 57th Street Beach was a hostile place, however, and they didn't want blacks on that beach. So, we went to the 63rd Street Beach because that was the "black" beach.

It's funny, I never remember calling my neighborhood the "Black Belt." The term "black" was just not an acceptable term at that time. There was a political maverick in the community by the name of Edgar G. Brown, and he was a great influence on my life. He was a bit of a vagabond type, and he would always stand on a soap box on the corner and talk about black people, economics and how the pen was mightier than the sword. I remember hearing him use that phrase, "black people," but it didn't sound correct to me. We didn't call each other "black people" because "negro" was the term of the day. It was like a foreign term, and we wondered why he was calling us "black" people. Of course, in the late 1960s the term "African-American" became popular, demonstrating how the labels for minority groups change based on the social politics of the time.

I went to Comiskey Park all the time and felt comfortable there. My father was a great baseball fan, and the Chicago American Giants of the Negro Leagues played there. Generally, we would go see the Negro Leagues more often than the White Sox. Our main interest was when the Chicago American Giants were back in town, because they played against the great Kansas City Monarchs, the Indianapolis Clowns, the Homestead Grays, the Pittsburgh Black Barons, and the Cuban-X Giants. I loved when Satchel Paige would come to town, as well as Josh Gibson and Cool Papa Bell.

I was also a big softball player when I was growing up, and there used to be great softball games at Comiskey Park. Businesses used to sponsor softball teams, and, in fact, the first guy I ever saw hit a softball out of Comiskey Park was Nate "Sweetwater" Clifton, who played for a team called the Cool Vent Awnings. He was a great, great athlete, and I saw him hit a 16-inch softball out of Comiskey Park straight down the left field line. Since I had a great interest in sports, I also used to go to the Chicago Cardinal games at Comiskey, with Charley Trippi and Ollie Matson, who was traded to the Los Angeles Rams for eleven players. I didn't think much of the Chicago Bears because they were the enemy — they would be the visitors at Comiskey Park. The Near North Side of Chicago was off limits in those days, and, in fact, I'm a White Sox fan today because Wrigley Field was such a negative place to go for blacks. My father took me there when I was 12 years old to see Jackie Robinson play for the Dodgers against the Cubs. I remember the hostility on the field and the booing in the stands, and those experiences definitely shaped my life.

I went to all Catholic schools growing up. I attended Corpus Christi Elementary School, which, at that time, was located at 49th and South Parkway. For my freshman year of high school, I was one of four black students selected by the nuns to go to St. Ignatius, a predominantly white school. As it turned out, St. Ignatius would not accept four black students at one time, so we got split up, and Richard Wilson and I went to St. Philip. It was a very difficult experience for me there, and although there were a few more black students at St. Philip, none were in my class other than Richard and myself. There was a smattering of blacks in the junior and senior classes, but very, very few people of color. It was, literally, the toughest year of my life — 1949.

It was also very, very tough commuting over to the school. I had never experienced this kind of behavior before, with the exception of going west across Wentworth Avenue into Bridgeport. There were always border skirmishes with that experience, and we always knew that was hostile territory — that was kind of understood. Up until that time, I had never experienced relationships with white people other than the merchants in my neighborhood. So, I wasn't prejudiced one way or another at that point in my life.

When I went to St. Philip, a school dominated by blue collar Irish, Italians and Poles, it was a wake-up call. I heard racial taunts and was threatened all the time there. I went out for the football team, and I remember some guy spit on me. I said, "Wow, you guys play football in a different way. When you are on the same side, you are not supposed to spit on each other." It was a traumatic experience that frightened me for many years afterward, because I had not witnessed that kind of hostility up-close.

I felt so negative about myself during that period of time. The nuns had thought that I would get a better educational experience by going there, and they viewed it as a step up for bright black kids to go to a "better" school. "Better" schools were, of course, white schools. I remember the priests, who were also our teachers, never really corrected the kids when they would say things to us or even get on their case about it. Unfortunately, it was a year of hell for me.

I had been at St. Philip maybe four or five days when I witnessed a fight out on the football field. A big Irish kid and a little Italian guy got into a fight, and the Italian kid broke a bottle and stuck it in this kid's neck and blood spewed everywhere. Since I was near the fight, blood got all over me. When I came home, my mother wondered if I had been in a fight. I told her, "You can't believe it, Mom, this school is crazy — these people are nuts!" I did go out for the basketball team because I was already 6'1" when I was a freshman. I was playing for the junior-varsity squad, and I was the only black kid on the team. We went down to St. Rita on the South Side and it was tough — when I would go up for a practice shot they would roll a ball under me so I would come down on the ball. It was awful. Those incidents, combined with all those threats and comments, made me fearful of going to school.

So, after that year of infamy, I said I had enough of it — I couldn't do it anymore. I went back to Corpus Christi High School at 46th and South Parkway and completed high school with all black students, and it was a much happier time for me. My experiences at St. Philip influenced me greatly, however. Even though I received a lot of athletic scholarships to white colleges, I turned them all down. Instead, in 1953, I went to Xavier College, an all-black school in New Orleans. My one year at St. Philip affected my decision. It was such a shock to my system, so I decided, "what do I need this grief for." Many of my friends who went to the University of Illinois were having the very problems that I feared — they had no social life and they couldn't go out anywhere. That was southern Illinois, and, at that time, it was like upper Mississippi. Of course, New Orleans, Louisiana was a segregated community, but the school was a kind of cocoon to live in at that time. In many ways, it was easier in a segregated society because you, at least, knew where you could go and where you could not go. There was no guesswork as to what was going on. Now, I'm not saying that was a wonderful alternative, but, at least, there was a restful feeling in one's mind that you weren't going to run into that kind of behavior pattern that I had run into at St. Philip. I did not want to be at some place I was not wanted, and not wanted because I was black.

I was at Xavier when *Brown vs. The Board of Education* happened in 1954. It was a celebration for us, and I remember being just wildly happy about it. There was no regard for black people at that time, and I don't know how one can describe such a feeling as being an invisible person — you just didn't seem to count. I felt great anger about the situation, but I didn't even recognize it as anger because I was so wrapped in fear. When it is a combination of fear and anger together, it is hard to separate where one ends and other starts.

Warner Saunders served as executive director of the Better Boys Foundation before beginning a 25-year career in television journalism at WMAQ-TV in Chicago.

On the Phone With Shelley Berman, c.1960
Photograph by Ed DeLuga *Chicago Sun-Times*

'CHICAGO IS EVERYTHING' SHELLEY BERMAN

I was born and raised on Chicago's West Side. I lived between Kedzie and Crawford Avenues and between 16th and 12th Streets. The only name I had for the neighborhood was the West Side. There was a *schvitz* there, a Russian bathhouse, at Roosevelt and Kedzie. My father used to take me to there — it was a great thing to go to a Russian bath for the day. They had what they called a *schmeiser*, who did the massaging. In that hot, hot steam room, and in that sauna with the wet heat — I couldn't breath at all — but that was the place!

On 16th Street and Sawyer Avenue there was an elementary school called Howland Elementary, and I still know the song for Howland. That was where I went during the 1930s for eight years — we didn't have middle school in those years. The neighborhood was primarily Jewish, but occasionally one of the "others" moved in. We would stare at them for a while until we became acquainted with the idea that they were okay, like the Husicks, who were Czechoslovakians, or the Prianos. Most of us lived in apartment buildings during those years. We didn't call them "apartments," we called them "flats."

We always played outside of and near our apartment. We played mumbly peg, rollevio, run-sheep-run, touch football, or almost any game. In those days we played all the time with other kids. We talked to each other, we did our homework together, and we got to know the kids on the block and in the neighborhood. We didn't sit there eating all day long and fattening ourselves like kids do today. We were outside, or we were sitting and "watching" radio. You didn't listen to radio, you "watched" radio, unless you had homework to do. Parents didn't indulge their kids in those days, and if you got a note from school you had a problem — it was a very different way of life when I was growing up. Incidentally, my first language at home was Yiddish, although I learned English when I got older. We lived with my grandparents and they spoke Yiddish, so, of course, everybody in the house spoke Yiddish. I also learned how to cook Jewish food.

As for the movies, we went to the Central Park Theater on 12th Street. Down closer to Independence Boulevard was the Road Theater, also known as the Independence Theater, and they showed a lot of Yiddish/Jewish movies there. A few doors before you got to the Central Park Theater was Fluky's Hot Dogs. At Fluky's, we learned that for $.15 you could have a hell of a meal. No hot dogs in the world compare with the Chicago hot dog, and Fluky's invented the great Chicago hot dog with everything on it — except ketchup. It was crazy to put ketchup on a hot dog and it still is wrong — in fact, it is anti-Semitic! You would put mustard and relish, they didn't have onions at the time, and they threw the French fries right in that same package — on the hot dog! It was wonderful, and I can still taste it — my mouth is watering just talking about it! Of course, you would also get a chocolate phosphate, with that mix of seltzer water and chocolate syrup, or you could get a red pop, since we didn't drink Coke or Dr. Pepper in those days.

Douglas Park was nearest to us, located near Albany and 16th Street. In winter, we went ice skating on the frozen lagoon there, and they had a place you could sit and get warmed-up. If you walked up Independence Boulevard past Roosevelt Road there was Garfield Park, with the beautiful conservatory. Everything was safe in those days, and you could sleep outside on the boulevards. I also remember the beautiful lilac bushes that were planted up and down the streets. To this day, all I want is to have lilac bushes, just for the wonderful smell, but you can't buy them in California. We would pick lilacs and bring them home to mom.

We used to have precinct captains during those days, and they would provide us with many services. My precinct captain arranged for me to get a transfer from Manley High school to Marshall, because there was a teacher who taught acting. Things didn't quite work out at the school. I took music there but the teacher never, ever looked up from her paper; I went to science class, but we never did an experiment. Eventually, I started cutting those classes because it was such a waste of time. Ultimately, I was kicked out of Marshall because of poor attendance, poor scholarship and poor citizenship! So, I had to go back to Manley High

School after one semester at Marshall. I wasn't so unhappy, because I found an English teacher at Manley whom I could study with, and I joined the choir and I loved that.

Before I graduated from high school I enlisted in the Navy during World War II, and thank God, the war ended and I got out on a medical discharge — mostly because the Navy was very interested in winning! I didn't know what to do with my life in the mid-1940s, so I decided that maybe I should find an easy school to go to, and that turned out to be the Goodman Theater, right behind the Art Institute of Chicago. So, I went there, but I had to talk my parents into letting me go. The GI Bill of Rights had just taken affect, but my father didn't want me to be an actor and my mother thought that I was crazy. It's true, she thought I was crazy! And they were worried that maybe I was a homosexual — because all actors are sissies! I don't know what they wanted me to be, but whatever it was, it sure wasn't acting. They knew that I was funny at parties, but I had no intention of being a comedian. None. I was funny in the Navy, but it never dawned on me that I could do this professionally. I thought that maybe I could become an actor.

At Goodman, I had a nice girlfriend by the name of Geraldine Page, and a good buddy just a half-year behind me by the name of Harvey Korman — it was like that. After a while I met this girl by the name of Sarah Herman, and it sounded like she ought to be Jewish, but she wasn't. She was from Providence High School, another place in Chicago. I could see right off that she wasn't Jewish — she was a Catholic girl, and she didn't know anything. She didn't even know how babies were born — she would learn eventually. She didn't know too much, but she was awfully cute. Meanwhile, I was hung up on Geraldine — I mean we were an item. Then, one summer, I found out that she got married. So, Sarah and I decided to get married in April 1947. Everybody knew it wouldn't last, but here we are still married after 58 years. I'm still Jewish and she became Jewish, and now she is more Jewish than I am!

So, in 1947, I didn't know what to do with myself, but around that time, I heard about this stock company in Woodstock, Illinois, called the Woodstock Players. I joined this company. Sarah came out with me and we lived in Woodstock, with all of us living on one floor of a rented house. There were people from Goodman in this company, including Lois Nettleton, who would do very well in our industry, a fellow by the name of Tom Bosley — and Geraldine Page. We were a non-equity group and did a play a week. We would open on a Thursday and would close on Sunday night and strike the set. The new set would be up by Monday morning and nobody ever had a day off. We were subsidized by the town of Woodstock, and were all making about $30 a week. We struggled together, and we played all the classics, including Shakespeare, Shaw and Ibsen. If we needed a wardrobe or a girl needed a special gown, all of a sudden a window would be missing its drape. When the show was over, we would hang it back in the window. We learned to do our own props, our own lighting, our own box office — we all did duties. You were a star one week and a flunky the next. The company was very successful, and the year I left the company a boy by the name of Paul Newman started at the Woodstock Opera House.

When that ended in the late 1940s, Sarah and I sought to make our fortune. I tried to be a social director at a hotel in Florida, but I was terrible at it. They fired me, and Sarah and I hitchhiked across the country to California. I finally wound up as an Arthur Murray dance instructor for a while, taking odd jobs and acting whenever I could. Then, Geraldine Page came out to do a movie called "Hondo" with John Wayne. She said to me, "What are you doing sitting on your ass?" She made me go to New York, a place that I hadn't been to. So, I tried my luck in and out of live theater, including "Goodyear Playhouse," "Philco Playhouse," and that sort of thing. While I was there I met a guy in the Stanley Wolf Players who did some summer stock in the Catskills — that was the closest I ever got to the Catskills! I was not a Catskill comic, ever, even though if you are Jewish you've got to be from New York. Well, I'm Jewish, but I'm from Chicago!

I'll tell you how I got started, and it certainly wasn't in the Catskills. I got a job as an actor, and we were touring with "Stalag 17." One of the guys in the cast, a nice looking kid by the name of Martin Landau, was part of that group. After the play closed we were looking for work and Marty was accepted by Actors Studio, which was thrilling for him — I was jealous because I had tried it and blew it. A Chicago group called Marty because they needed somebody to fill a spot vacated by one of the players, so he said, "I have a job, but there's another fellow here, maybe you can use him." So, I joined the Compass Players.

When I got there a lot of these kids were younger than me, and it bothered me that I was still struggling and here they were doing things. I was wondering if I was ever going to get started in life because I hadn't made it yet. I met Barbara Harris there, and I also met another girl who really should have done something with her hair, but she was marvelous — Elaine May — and a skinny, pale kid whose name was Mike Nichols. I also met a fellow by the name of Paul Sills, who loved to intellectualize things into oblivion. He just loved to intellectualize, and he and Mike Nichols would go round and round. But I learned what that was: it was not just oblivion, it was creation.

Now, in those days, I thought that you got on stage to be funny. So, I tried that a couple of times, to everyone's dismay, including my own. No, that wasn't the purpose. You get out there and you improvise, and when you improvise you're not just trying to "out funny" everybody out there, or get all the laughs. You're out there to communicate with each other, and make it all happen together. I learned this within the first few weeks there, and I realized — my God — this is what Uta Hagen had been teaching for so long now: play your action and everything will take care of itself.

The Compass Players was located on the South Side at a place called The Deck, or The Dock — we never got that correct. It could have been either place, because at one time you would see an "e" there and another time you would see an "o" there. It was just a little bar. These people were fabulous, and we did things together that I never dreamed I could do. I found myself capable of improvising and playing something quite seriously and getting laughter as a result. The technique was quite extraordinary, but it was exactly what Uta Hagen had been teaching me for the longest time: play your action, play your needs — don't go out there just to act, go out there for a reason. Well, in a month or two, I had it. Still, however, I was driven because I was a little older than they were by about four years, and I was getting scared that I hadn't made a career for myself — and I was coming up on thirty years old. I was scared to death, but I knew that I had the talent and the will. So, I began to get along and work with these marvelous people. I never stopped admiring them — never. Working with them was such a pleasure and such a gift given to me. I still sit in awe thinking of what I watched them do and what I was part of.

I was with Compass Players almost three years, until they left Chicago in 1957 and moved to St. Louis. I decided to stay in Chicago. I didn't know what I was going to do with my life in Chicago, but I knew that I had to do something. Around that time, I had developed some "phone calls" where I could play the thing by myself. That was the technique. It wasn't a gimmick — it never occurred to me. However, it started me as a monologist, although I didn't realize that was happening to me. Now, as far as I was concerned these were marvelous phone calls, but what the hell am I going to do with them? You can't do this in a nightclub with people smoking and drinking! You've got to have these big, strong powerful jokes — that's the way the comedians who I had seen worked in those places.

Then, one day, I heard about a fellow named Mort Sahl. He worked in a place called Mister Kelly's on Rush Street, so I went there to see this young man work. I saw the thrust of his efforts — he was working within certain limits, and he was improvising, finding his way, but he knew which way he was going each time — and the shows were different each time. I see this marvelous creativity taking place before me, and he didn't have to tell hard jokes. All he had to do was be bright and original — and he was.

I first performed at Mister Kelly's soon after I saw Mort. I wangled an audition and performed a few phone calls, and they hired me at $350 a week with an option for four weeks. My god, I was earning money! About a year later, since Mort and I were friends, he talked me into doing an album. He said that I should record my show with his record company. The album was called "Inside Shelley Berman" — and it was a phenomenal hit. My God did it sell! Well, pretty soon, I was working in all the places that you are supposed to work, including The Hungry I in San Francisco and the Blue Angel in New York. These were the key places for performers. When the record hit, all of a sudden, people I was opening for were now opening for me! It was exciting and splendid. Chicago is such a key in my life. Chicago is everything.

Shelley Berman has taught writing at the University of Southern California for over twenty years. He appears regularly on HBO's "Curb Your Enthusiasm."

Waitress at Wimpy's, 1 N. Clark, 1957
Photograph by Rubin Goldman

FINDING HIS WAY RICH MELMAN

I would never want to give up my childhood in the Logan Square neighborhood. I loved it. I mean, if you wanted to play ball, there were literally thirty kids on the block who you could play ball with, and we would organize our own games. Everything we wanted to do was within walking distance. You didn't need a car in the city. In fact, I didn't even have a bike until we moved to the suburbs.

My favorite restaurant in Logan Square was the Terminal Restaurant. I remember that my parents would take me there on Sunday nights and my favorite thing to eat was the cream of chicken soup. Then, afterwards, right next to the restaurant, was the actual terminal for the elevated trains. They had this big newsstand with comic books there, and my father would always buy me one. I was an avid comic book collector, and on Friday afternoons, from about 4 to 6 o'clock, our ritual was to gather our comics together and meet with the other kids to trade. Afterwards, I would go home, have dinner, and be in bed by about 8:30 because I couldn't wait to read my new comics. Then, I'd read them until I fell asleep — next to my brother who shared the bed! My dad didn't like me to have horror comics or anything like that, but I loved Archie and Captain Marvel comics. I also loved it when *Mad* magazine came out — it was so revolutionary. A kid in my neighborhood named Michael Stone showed me my first *Mad* — I couldn't believe what a wild thing it was — and couldn't wait to get the next one.

I was a very, very good marble player in those days. We played everywhere: in the school yard, in grass around our house, and on the sidewalk where you would put "one up." I was just a real good marble player and I had jars and jars and jars of marbles, but I have no idea whatever happened to them. I am sure that my mother threw them out when we moved. I also remember the Duncan yo-yo man, and I loved yo-yos. I wasn't any expert, but I could "walk the cradle," "walk the dog," and go "over the falls."

On Saturdays, I remember listening to "Archie Andrews and Jughead" on the radio in the morning, and then going to the movies at the Armitage or Bell Theater and watching 25 cartoons in the afternoon. I also remember when our upstairs neighbors, the Myerson's, were the first family to get a television — a Zenith round screen in a big console — and once in a while we would go up to watch Milton Berle. It was amazing to me. We didn't get a television until two years later, and I guess that we couldn't afford one because my folks went through some hard times. I always wanted to be invited up to the Myerson's place, but they didn't invite us too much, so I just saw one or two shows in those first couple of years.

I loved sports, and I was lucky because I got to play with the older guys all the time. When I was ten, I was playing sports with the guys who were 12 and older. Early on, I got really interested in athletics, and I was pretty good for my age. In fact, I was one of the better athletes around, and the older guys always let me play with them. I started out being a pinch runner or picking up the bases, or just doing things that they needed to get done — then they would let me play.

As for Wrigley Field, I remember going there with a young, blind boy in our neighborhood who was a couple of years younger than me named Ronnie Beister. I liked Ronnie — we just hit it off — and we would pal around together. His mother was a waitress, and every once in a while she would get tickets to a Cubs game. So, if I would take Ronnie, she would get us the tickets. It was just a thrill, and I would go to the ballpark around four or five times a year. When we went to a game, we would always get there around 10:30 in the morning — and we stayed for everything. In those days, the players would come down after the game to sign autographs, so we would wait to see them. So, we would get to the ballpark at 10:30 a.m. and come home after 5:00 p.m. I remember that I loved

Richie Ashburn. You see, I was a leadoff hitter too — and my name was Richie — so I just loved Richie Ashburn. I remember waiting and waiting and waiting, and he finally gave me an autograph. I also got Willie Mays' autograph. It was unbelievable, and I have great memories of those times. I only went to Comiskey Park once — to watch Ted Williams and the Red Sox play. I hated the White Sox — you are either a Sox fan or a Cub fan.

In my junior year of high school we moved to Skokie. I was going to Kelvyn Park High School and really wanted to finish there. After all, I was playing ball there, and I had all my friends there — I grew up in the neighborhood. My parents decided to move to Skokie because the Logan Square neighborhood had become pretty tough. It had gotten very gang-oriented, although not like gangs today. There were no shootings, but there was a lot of fist fighting and problems in the neighborhood. Also, because I had a younger brother, they just wanted a better place for us to grow up. After we moved I did keep going to Kelvyn Park for awhile, even though they had a law at the time requiring transfer students to pay as much as $400 in order to live in the suburbs and go to a Chicago Public School. I didn't have a car, so I had to hitchhike from Skokie to Peterson Avenue, take a bus down to Wrightwood, and then walk over to high school. It was really a trek.

I ended up continuing at Kelvyn Park for only a couple of months. I wanted to keep going back, but it just became impossible. So, begrudgingly, I went to Niles East High School. I didn't want to, particularly since I started new during my senior year. It was hard and I didn't like it. I didn't really know anybody there, although I had met some of the kids who played on the basketball team in a league that I tried out for at the end of my junior year. I did make the varsity team at Niles East and played well, but I was like a stranger to them. Eventually it got to be passable, but my heart was always at Kelvyn Park. I went back there many times — whenever I had a chance. If I had a free weekend, I would call up my friends and go back. It was difficult to adapt to Niles East because the kids dressed better, it was more competitive socially, and the kids were wealthier. As a result, I didn't date, I was just sort of bashful with the girls and I was a very average student in high school.

I graduated from Niles East in 1960 and then I went to Roosevelt University for a year. I was a horrible student, and I remember my father asking, "Why don't you just quit?" My first semester, I got two Cs and two Ds. My father, who had put away about $2,000 for me, said, "Why waste it on college? Why not take it and do something with it?"

Well, that's when I thought seriously about the restaurant business. I started working in restaurants when I was about 13 or 14 years old, but I never loved it or thought much about it as a career. My dad, Morrie Melman, co-owned a number of restaurants with his brother, the first being a cafeteria across from the Civic Opera House on Wacker Drive. That started them in the restaurant business, and then they opened up two more restaurants: Ricky's on Roosevelt and Crawford and another Ricky's on Division and California. Eventually, my father and uncle split up the businesses; my uncle took the restaurant on Division and California and my father kept the one on the West Side. Not long after that my dad sold his restaurant and opened one up on Belmont and Broadway, but then sold that one and opened up Mr. Ricky's on Skokie Boulevard and Gross Point Road. He always had one place, never two at a time.

I was a decent worker at my father's restaurants, and I also worked at Henry's Drive-In selling Good Humor Bars — just a bunch of different places. I remember one time, when I was about 19 years old and working for my father, I was on a softball team that was playing for a championship at Grant Park. Although I went in to work early that day, I knew that I would be leaving at 11 a.m. for the game. Well, it was a very busy day at Ricky's at Broadway and Belmont, and I told the manager that I would be back in a couple of hours. We won a doubleheader to win the championship, and at about 3:00 p.m. I came back to the restaurant with all the guys. My father was livid because he thought I had been irresponsible, and it really bothered me. I remember one of the restaurant cashiers said to me, "You are a good worker when you want to be, but you don't seem focused or serious." I was still in my wild time and wasn't ready to settle down at that age. So, I started to sell Fuller brushes, and it was just awful going door-to-door. I realized then that I wasn't very good at asking for favors, but I was much better doing favors and servicing people's needs and wants. As a result of those experiences, I became very serious about the restaurant business.

So, I started to read all I could about the business. I attended seminars and focused on making a career in the restaurant industry. Within a couple of years, I started liking it, and I really thought that I wanted to be a partner with my father and his partner, Lou Greenberg. By the time I was in my mid-20s, I was a manager at Mr. Ricky's and working very hard. I had given up sports and my social life to dedicate most of my time to being successful in the restaurant business. I approached my father and Mr. Greenberg about being a partner with them, and they said that they wanted to think about it. At that time, I would have been happy if they would have sold me 2% of the business. I had saved up about $10,000 and was willing to buy a piece of the restaurant. They sat me down and said, "We want to see you more settled and married before we bring you into the business." I was really disappointed — I didn't even have time to go out on dates because I was so focused on learning the business. I couldn't believe that they didn't appreciate what I would bring to the venture. I remember going back to work and realizing that something had changed in me. So, over the next couple of weeks, I made the decision to do something away from them, either on my own or with other partners. I wanted a future and to be a part of something.

I met Jerry Orzoff the first time in 1967, and a couple of years later we met again and hit it off. He said that he wanted to partner on opening a restaurant, and I agreed that it would be a good idea. That led to R.J. Grunt's (named after my oldest son) in 1972, and then to the creation of Lettuce Entertain You Enterprises, and the rest is history. The funny part is that R.J. Grunts, my first restaurant, is on Dickens Street, the same street I grew up on in Logan Square. It was such an omen to me when we found that location. That half block at Dickens and Lincoln Park West now honors me with the name Richard Melman Way.

Rich Melman is president and CEO of Lettuce Entertain You Enterprises, which includes such popular restaurants as Scoozi!, Maggiano's and Shaw's Crab House.

Jack Rosenberg at Comiskey Park, c.1958

THE DREAM JOB JACK ROSENBERG

I was born in Pekin, which is in central Illinois and at that time had a population of about 20,000 residents. As I look back, it was one of the most pleasurable periods of my life. It was a great place to grow up, and it seemed like we knew everybody. There was a lot of spirit around the town.

I got to my senior year at Pekin High School and was nominated to run for Student Council President. There were four of us who ran: two boys and two girls. At that point in time, in 1943, I was the only Jewish student in a high school of 1,300. I remember that there was a $10 limit on campaign expenses, so I went to my cousin at his hardware store and said, "Could you give me a little break on paint? I have 500 or 600 signs that I am going to make, and I can only spend $10." My cousin said, "I am going to give you the paint, but keep in mind that you will never be elected student council president at that high school. Even as good as you are in school — no way!" It was a three-day campaign and I kissed babies, shook hands, and got to know everybody at the school. It was a great experience, and I won.

After the school year, I was getting ready for summer vacation. I always wanted to be a newspaperman, and all my testing showed that I would be pretty good at it, so I decided to take a shot at the newspaper business. I walked up the street and went into the office of the *Pekin Daily Times*, one of the great small town newspapers in America. As luck would have it, Mr. F.F. McNaughton, the publisher, was standing in front of the office of the *Times*. I introduced myself, and he said, "Jack Rosenberg — weren't you just elected student council president?" I said, "Yes, sir." He said, "You know, my son Dean is at West Point now. He was student council president." I said, "I know Dean, he was a couple years ahead of me." He said, "I will tell you this much, if you're Jewish and good enough to be elected council president, you're good enough to work at the *Pekin Times*. You can start Monday at $16 a week." That was like winning the lottery.

After working my way up to sports editor there, I went into the Navy in June of 1944 — D-Day week. In 1945, I was just about ready to go to the South Pacific when they dropped the Atomic Bomb, so they canceled our departure and the rest is history. I came back and went to work at the *Peoria Journal-Star*, the largest downstate Illinois newspaper. While I was there, I was lucky enough to win two NCAA awards as tops in the nation for college baseball reporting for papers over 100,000 circulation.

I spent five years there, and I eventually got a chance to meet Jack Brickhouse, who was already well-established in Chicago. Jack and my boss, Kenny Jones, sports editor of the *Journal*, both were great friends of Arch Ward of the *Chicago Tribune*, the greatest sports editor — ever. They set me up with an interview at the *Tribune*. What an experience — here I am, in my mid-20s, talking to Arch Ward, and sitting in his glassed-in office in Tribune Tower in Chicago. It was fantastic, and we talked for an hour.

When we got done, he said, "You know, you come highly recommended, and I'm impressed with what I hear from you. I've got a job for you at the *Tribune* with me. It starts in three weeks at $100 a week." My face fell, and he said, "Is there a problem?" I said, "Yes sir, I'm making $110 in Peoria." He said, "Well, let me explain something. See that man out there. He used to be at the *Philadelphia Inquirer* and he is making $100 a week. Over there, another reporter from a big city paper, and he is making $100 a week here. You see, it's not the starting salary. It's if you are in the right place when the lightning strikes. I suspect that you will be. I have a feeling about that." I said, "My problem is that my mother is widowed and I want to bring her to Chicago with me. So, ten dollars a week means a lot to me." He said, "You go home and think it over, and let me know." So, I had one of the most agonizing train rides in my life. I had always wanted to work for the *Tribune* sports department ever since 5th grade in Pekin, and now my dreams had been realized — but I couldn't do it. So, I wrote Arch Ward a letter in which I noted that I was overwhelmed with meeting him in person, and the fact that he offered me a job, but that I was going to respectfully decline. I received a letter back from him by registered mail. He wrote that he had great respect for me because of my loyalty to my newspaper and to my mother, and then he wrote, "While we have a policy to start everyone at the same salary, if you will give me three months, I am going to try to work around it so that no one will get upset, and you will be getting a little more money." I thought that this was praise from Caesar.

While I was waiting to hear from Mr. Ward, Jack Brickhouse called me up. He said, "Hey, kid, I know that you want to work for the Tribune Company. My right hand man just left to take over the Springfield bureau of WGN. I have a job open, and you would be a natural. I'd love to have you here, and you will be with the broadcasting division of the Tribune." I said, "Mr. Brickhouse, I've never been around television or radio. I am strictly a newspaper man." He responded, "You know what, Jack, no problem. Come up and visit with me and let's talk it over." So, the next day I was on the train to Chicago, and then Wilmette. I sat down with Jack Brickhouse in his home and we talked for hours. Three weeks later, I was working for the Tribune Company, but with WGN Television and Radio — at $85.00 a week!

Looking back, the early days with the Chicago Cubs and Chicago White Sox were wonderful. I was the producer and writer for the baseball coverage, and as Jack used to say, if he ever said anything clever I wrote it. We wound up with one of the greatest sports departments ever. I would sit there with my portable typewriter writing in the background, and Jack was so good that he could throw the stuff in and you would never know it was being written. Except, as the years went by, a lot of people listened for that typewriter sound. Of course, we were all part of something special — we weren't just subservient to him or what he was doing — those things you never forget. Jack was one of the ushers when I married my wife Mayora in 1956. He had never been to a Jewish wedding ceremony before, and at the conclusion of the ceremony the groom steps on a glass and shatters it for good luck. When I did it Jack jumped about three feet in the air, and during the rest of his years, he went around telling people that he thought somebody had taken a shot at him.

Generally, I would get to the ballpark three hours early, minimum, before every game and hang around. The great John P. Carmichael of the *Chicago Daily News* once told me that he never took notes while he was interviewing, but as soon as the interview was over, whatever was really important had stuck with him, and he would make notes to himself. This way, he didn't intimidate anyone he was talking to. I would hang around the dugouts, the clubhouses, and the front offices, and by the time each game started, I had those little human interest items. Statistics were given to us by the ballclub public relations people, but my job was to get human interest stories that would fit well into the telecast. We did that for years and years and years. Starting from that, I branched out into producing and editing, and I wound up during most of my years running the day-to-day operation of what was to become the greatest sports department in the United States.

Even at the beginning, in the mid-1950s, it seemed to me all the fans and the media were resigned to the fact that the Cubs were never going to win. Yet, here I was sitting alongside somebody whose disposition was so "sunny." I really thought that Jack, in his own mind, was never looking at a loser. We knew all these people, personally, so they were not only players, they were also friends. In those days it was a different era all together. Year in and year out, the Cubs would lose. Spring training would start, you would say that this was going to be good season, but then the same things would happen. But in Jack's mind, they were all winners.

During the 1950s, Irv Kupcinet joined Jack as the color man on the Chicago Bears radio broadcast on WGN-AM. During the first broadcast, Jack asked Kup if he would need any help lining up half-time interviews. Kup said that he thought he was set with guests, and just before the half, the doors of the booth opened and in walked Carmen Basilio, who had just won the middleweight boxing championship, Bob Hope and former President Harry Truman. So, after that day Jack figured that Kup really didn't need any help getting guests for interviews.

Another great broadcaster was Jack Quinlan — who possibly had the greatest voice of any announcer. He was just tremendous, and I really enjoyed working with him on football. He was very meticulous about what he did, and I still recall, in particular, his "spotting boards" for Big Ten football when I produced those games. He had so many notes on his spotting boards that they were three-deep! Jack's board was always full of little insights which he would drop into his commentary as he went along. He was a tremendous broadcaster and was really just getting started when, in 1965, at the age of 38, he ran into the back of a semitrailer in Mesa, Arizona and was killed.

Matching Jack Quinlan with Lou Boudreau turned out to be a stroke of genius — they were beautiful together. Lou was one of those "part of the family" broadcasters, in that everybody felt like he was sitting in their living room while they listened to him. Grammatically, he may have missed a few English classes, but his knowledge of baseball was so penetrating that you could put him against any analyst, then or now, and he would give a good account of himself. Lou was a Hall of Fame shortstop with the Cleveland Indians, and in 1948 reached a pinnacle when they played and beat the Boston Braves in the World Series. I still remember using videotape years later of Boudreau sitting in a convertible with his wife, Della, going down the main street in Cleveland and being honored.

Vince Lloyd was another phenomenal broadcaster and a "hale fellow well met." He had the pear-shaped tones and a nice, rich, deep, resonant voice. During one period of time we had Jack Brickhouse, Vince Lloyd and me in the booth, with Jack in the middle. Vince was of Lebanese descent, I am Jewish, and Jack used to like to tell people that, for him, it was like sitting on the Gaza Strip. Vince, Jack, Lou and I were like brothers, and we did everything together. We traveled together, and socialized with each other's families. Those guys always looked for the positive side of sports. Vince was doing television when he was offered the radio deal with Boudreau, and he had trepidation about leaving television, which they all do. But he decided to do it, and it turned out to be a long association — Vince and Lou were a great team. They didn't look at baseball as if the world was dependent upon it. It was a fun thing — it wasn't life or death.

Bob Elson was another of the all-time greats, and a Hall of Fame broadcaster. It was Bob Elson who got Jack Brickhouse started in Chicago in 1940. Jack always kept the original telegram that Bob had sent him. It read, "I'm bringing you up here. When they interview you make sure you tell them that you've done a lot of baseball."

I remember the day when Bob was filling in on a radio show after the ball games on WGN. The Houston Open was being played that weekend, and Bob used to keep a television on his desk to monitor anything that might be happening. This particular Sunday, with Bob making phone calls to his friends in between everything else, he missed the fact that the Houston Open had been rained out, and the network was running a replay of the previous year's Houston Open. Earlier in the day I had been at Wrigley Field, and, of course, knew that the tournament was off until Monday. So, I'm listening to Elson doing his sports wrap-up — he liked to be as dramatic as he could — and suddenly he shouts, "Flash! Flash! Here's a flash from Houston! Lee Trevino has just won the Houston Open!" Well, he had won it, but he had won it the year before. Boy, I almost drove off the road. I mean, this was beautiful!

Jack Brickhouse and I were very close and I would have difficulty finding the words to describe him both as a broadcaster and as a friend. He was the centerpiece of what happened with WGN Sports. Generally, he and I have been credited by a lot of kind people as being the architects of what would become this billion dollar sports department, but Jack really was the one who attracted all of us to come here to WGN. He learned the ropes in Peoria and was very proud of that. He literally became an institution here. He always seemed to find time for a "hello" for everybody, helped countless broadcasters get started and would always make that call if somebody needed help. Jack just had a cheery disposition. You could find him in the 7th Inning of game two of a doubleheader — when all the rest of us were dragging and could hardly wait for the games to be over — he was just as excited as he was in the first inning of the first game.

You know, for somebody like me, to come out of Peoria, IL and to suddenly be mingling with these greats, whom I had only heard about and read about — this was a revelation for me. From the beginning, I didn't have a job where you looked at the clock and wondered what time you could go home, or when you could get your vacation. None of that. It was the same for the rest of the people with whom I worked. We really loved our jobs, and we all thought that we had "dream" jobs.

Jack Rosenberg retired from broadcasting in 1999 after 45 years with WGN television and radio.

1 LIFE IN THE NEIGHBORHOODS

In the years following World War II, Chicago's neighborhoods slowly began to change. Many ethnic enclaves and parish affiliations, some existing for over a hundred years, began to give way to social and economic forces. It was a time of transition, and for many Chicago residents new neighborhoods were in their future, some moving north until they pushed into the suburbs of Lincolnwood, Skokie and Niles, and others moving south to Oak Lawn, Evergreen Park and Park Forest. And the numbers were dramatic — between 1940 and 1960, Skokie's population grew from 7,172 to 59,364, and in Park Forest, an entirely privately planned community, the population grew from 3,000 acres of open land to over 30,000 residents. Other suburbs saw similar growth, and with the aid of the automobile and newly constructed expressways, Chicago began to undergo a fundamental population shift.

For those who left the city, the suburbs offered a chance to own a home for the first time, better schools for their children to attend, and hope for a better quality of life. For those who stayed in Chicago, life gradually became more complicated as the city struggled with the social upheaval that the 1960s brought. But in the years before these changes took place, life continued to follow the patterns established decades earlier — a good life characterized by close-knit families, quiet neighborhoods and simple pleasures.

The Old Neighborhood

Life in Chicago was still pretty simple in 1950. Most neighborhoods had everything you needed close by: a school, church, library, grocery, tavern, park, dime store, movie theater and a funeral home — and you could get to most of these places by walking. The days of the ice man were almost over, but the rags-old-iron man could still be seen in the alley, as well as the milkman and an occasional knife sharpener. Neighbors knew and looked out for each other, families ate and socialized together and kids kept themselves busy with a minimum of adult supervision — all day long if necessary.

The city's neighborhood shopping districts still offered an amazingly diverse range of products and services, something that would change with the influence of the one-stop supermarkets. For customers who were used to the "Old World" quality of the ethnic markets, the switch from independently-owned stores to the big chains was not necessarily a welcome one. For generations, workers in ethnic bakeries would rise as early as 2:00 a.m. to begin the process of preparing breads, rolls and sweets to be ready for the first customers at 6:00 a.m. In each enclave the favorites were different: Bohemians baking kolacky, Slovenians baking potica and Polish baking babka. In neighborhood butcher shops the same quality and choices could be found: homemade liver sausage, frankforters, blood sausage and even live chickens and fish. Neighborhood groceries could also have a local twist, each stocking ethnic favorites to meet the tastes of the neighborhood, as well as the essentials: milk, bread and eight-ounce Cokes.

Every neighborhood also had its own army of small businesses, including shoemakers, upholsterers, locksmiths and repair shops. For many Chicagoans, as each owner retired or went out of business the absence didn't register as a loss, but rather as evidence of just how unnecessary they were in the "new" and "modern" world that was emerging. Who needs to fix anything? Just buy a new one — a better one.

But for older Chicagoans, particularly those who lived through and were shaped by the Depression and World War II, the "Old World" ways of the neighborhood were just fine. This generation of Chicagoans has always been known for their common sense, frugality and the pride they took in homeownership. Hard work was a virtue to them, and not working was a sin. Domestic chores were attacked with vigor, and despite the availability of new products to make life easier, many still washed and wrung their laundry by hand, used a push mower for their lawns and grew and canned their own fruit and vegetables.

Religion was still a powerful influence in the lives of Chicagoans, with entire communities built around strong church, parish and synagogue affiliations. For many Catholics, daily or weekly masses, in Latin until 1962, were a regular part of life, as well as church-sponsored festivals, sports leagues, dances and school activities. For members of the Jewish faith the role of the synagogue was equally central to their lives, with many children receiving religious instruction after attending public elementary and high schools. Church carnivals were welcome sights to members of any faith, and were usually held in parking lots next to the schools. Kids liked the Tilt-A-Whirl and other rides, while parents and the older crowd could get a beer and enjoy a game of chance, including different forms of gambling — something banned from carnivals today.

While the neighborhood clergyman would help with issues of the soul, it was the local precinct captain who helped with everything else. Political power may have rested in the hands of Mayors Edward Kelly, Martin Kennelly and Richard J. Daley during the era, but it was the precinct captain who got things done. When residents needed junk hauled away or potholes fixed, it was the captain who made sure the problem was addressed by the city. And if the city didn't act fast enough, he did it himself, because he needed every vote on election day.

Taverns were a fixture in every neighborhood in the city, and during the late '40s and early 1950s the phone book averaged about 6000 listings. The names could be colorful, like Junior's Radio Inn, Club Whirlabout and Valente's House of Nickelodeons, or simply named after the owner, like Jim's, Jack's and Joe's. The city's taverns and did more than just serve alcohol — they were meeting places for neighbors, friends and coworkers and offered regulars a range of activities to keep them coming back, like food, juke box music (some even had their own organists), bowling alleys, interesting surrounds (one advertised "original and unique Alaskan decorations"), television and air conditioning. Different forms of gambling were also a diversion in taverns in these days, like punch cards, also known as tavern cards, which were sold from behind the bar. The cards offered the buyer a chance to win cash or prizes by punching-through a slot using a push key, with a small piece of paper inside the slot indicating the prize.

Before automobile ownership was widespread, Chicagoans relied on trains, buses and streetcars to get them around their neighborhood and the city. Chicago's transportation system was one of the nation's best, and residents, particularly children, loved the old streetcars and "L" trains. But after World War II, when car makers began manufacturing new automobiles again, ownership was on the rise — while public transportation ridership was falling. In an effort to hold on to its ridership, the Chicago Transportation Authority (CTA) sought to modernize their system to compete the with the popularity of the automobile. This meant the old streetcars, which were a fixture in the neighborhoods for years, began to slowly be replaced with electric and diesel buses, which were seen by the CTA as the future of public transit. Making matters worse, a series of dramatic accidents during the 1950s turned public opinion against the streetcars, the worst coming on May 25, 1950, when 33 people were killed after a horrifying collision with a gasoline truck. The final "Green Hornet" streetcar ran in Chicago on June 21, 1958, with the shells of the old cars retrofitted for use on the city's elevated lines.

Change in Chicago's neighborhoods was not just limited to the streetcars, however, and each year a little more of old Chicago was lost to "progress." Buildings were torn down to make way for expressways and parking lots; corner stores and groceries yielded to new supermarkets; and streets made of pavers and brick were replaced with concrete and asphalt. For many residents, the Chicago neighborhoods of their youth would never look the same again, and it was felt as a great loss. For others, the changes were a positive sign and couldn't come fast enough. Many of the most impatient residents headed out of the city to new neighborhoods and a new way of life — to the suburbs.

The New Neighborhoods

In the years following World War II, as large numbers of returning veterans sought homes or apartments, there was a tremendous shortage of housing in Chicago. The city's rental market was pushed to its limits, which left many residents living in cramped, small apartments not meant for large families. In Bronzeville and other African American neighborhoods, the need for more housing was particularly great due to years of discrimination in the city's real estate market. This housing shortage, combined with the rise of automobile ownership and a growing American economy, led to the rapid development of the suburbs in Chicagoland.

New development was focused mainly in areas where large tracts of open land existed. In older and more established suburbs like Evanston and Oak Park there was little land left for new construction, but all around the city's border, in suburbs like Skokie, Oak Lawn and Evergreen Park, there were thousands of acres of undeveloped land perfect for large scale subdivisions. Previously, developments in these locations would have been considered impractical, but the wave of automobile ownership and expressway construction made it possible. Soon, new development would push farther and farther out — beyond Cook County into DuPage, Lake and Will Counties.

Most Chicagoans hadn't ventured out to the suburbs much before the 1950s, occasionally going to Arlington Park Racetrack, Ravinia Park, Brookfield Zoo or one of the many cemeteries and picnic grounds that ringed the city. This would all change as suburban development increased and enticed city residents to the new attractions previously unavailable in Chicago. As shopping centers, miniature golf courses, drive-in theaters, go-cart tracks and driving ranges appeared around the area, residents began venturing out to the suburbs more and more. Eventually, as ex-Chicagoans/new suburbanites began relating stories of their homes to old neighbors and friends, they felt much more comfortable with the idea of living in the new communities.

Not that Chicagoans needed much encouragement to move, particularly those frustrated in their attempts to find any housing at all in the city. There was very little residential construction going on, while the suburbs saw incredible growth and development. For growing "Baby Boom" families trying to live in Chicago it was particularly difficult, because in many cases parents had to share bedrooms with their children, or have kids sleep in the living or dining rooms. In fact, it wasn't uncommon for unscrupulous landlords to force desperate tenants into taking an apartment "furnished," which really meant buying furniture they did not want — just to have the opportunity to rent. Issues like these made the suburbs very appealing, and for many longtime renters the chance to finally own a home was "a dream come true."

Soon, the floodgates would open, and the land that for generations hosted farm fields and pastures would be transformed into an extension of the city.

The Choice: The "Good Life" or Staying Behind

The new suburban neighborhoods looked and functioned radically different from the old ones in the city. The idea of neighborhood self-containment, which for generations guided Chicago development, was abandoned in the suburbs. Instead, most communities were built around the concept of automobile travel, which meant you needed a car to live there — these cities were not planned with walking or public transportation as a priority. So, rather than walking to a series of local businesses spread out over a neighborhood, residents would drive to a single shopping "center" where they could find everything they needed in one location.

The quality of life in these neighborhoods would also be different, mainly because the new suburban homes were so different from the old homes Chicagoans moved from. Residents didn't need to go outside in the summer to cool off anymore, because they had insulated homes with air conditioning. They didn't need to go shopping as often, because they had roomy kitchens with much more storage space. They didn't need to go to a park or playground to be outdoors, because they had large backyards to cook out and play in. Perhaps the biggest change of all was privacy. Unlike the life of an apartment dweller, where privacy was never an option, these new neighborhoods could offer a much quieter life — even solitude if desired.

Thousands of families would move to the suburbs in the '50s, each for different reasons, but most felt that the old neighborhoods could never adapt to the "modern" world that was taking shape. The old homes seemed hopelessly outdated, each filled with dark wood, push button light switches and other symbols of the past. To these Chicagoans, bungalows and workingman's cottages would be impossible to "update," and they would be the first to leave the city.

For those who remained behind, it was almost unimaginable leaving their neighborhoods — it was home — it was the only world they knew. Their friends, churches and favorite stores and restaurants were all still there — at least for a little while.

Page 24: *View of the Loop From*
Near North Side Rooftop, c.1950

The Old Neighborhood

Southwest Side Bartenders, c.1950

South Side Churchgoer, c.1950
Photograph by Lorenzo Stalling

Beat Cop on West Madison Street, Austin, c. 1950

"Fireman, Engine Company 19," c.1950
Photograph by Rubin Goldman

Organ Grinder Sam Canzona, 1953
Photograph by Joe Kordick *Chicago Sun-Times*

Ice Man, 1952
Photograph by Dave Mann *Chicago Sun-Times*

Food Vendors, c.1950
Photograph by James Numata
Japanese American Service Committee Legacy Center

West Garfield Park Residents, c.1950

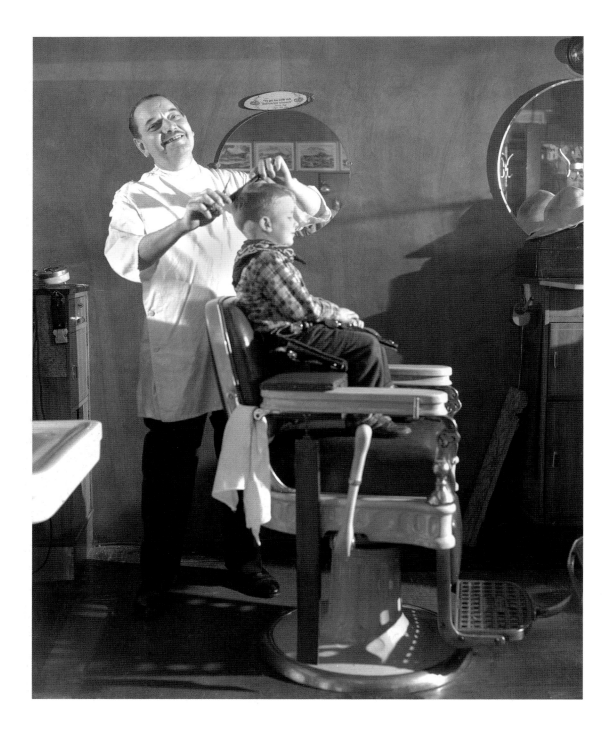

Charles Schriddler, North Side Barber, c.1955
Photograph by William Hugh

South Side Youth on Rooftop, c.1950
Photograph by Lorenzo Stalling

'We All Worked Hard' | Jim O'Connor

In 1948, I was in grade school, at Little Flower on the Southwest Side. The thing that I remember most about that period, in the Catholic schools anyway, was that tuition was $1 a month. When the monthly payment came due, every kid I knew got the same lecture from his mother or father about their sacrifice in order to keep you in a Catholic school. It was never lost on you that there was an expectation there, one that meant that you had to do your homework, that you had to be on time, and that you could never be absent. That $1 was viewed as a sacrifice — whether or not it was. It was a very common theme in the Catholic schools back then — the church subsidized it and the nuns were only making a dollar a day. Of course, it was a great way to build up a value system as to what things were important, and everything revolved around "doing the work, being on time, and never being absent." I'm sure it was also true for the public schools, but the added incentive for the kids in the Catholic schools was that somebody was paying for it.

Now, no kids could afford to have their own cars back then. In my senior year at St. Ignatius, where we had 200 kids in the graduating class, there were only two guys who had cars. One of them was the son of a mechanic, and he had an old "rattletrap" that would fall apart all the time. The other kid had a car that we were absolutely convinced was "hot." The guy had a DA haircut slicked back, and everyone just figured that it was either stolen or a car that he shouldn't have had. Of course, these kids had to park down the street because the Jesuits would never permit anybody to have that sort of luxury at the age of 17 or 18. I mean, it was just unheard of at that age! Until you were a senior, nobody even got a car to take a date out — you went on a streetcar. And hitchhiking was very common for kids. In fact, the street corners were laden with kids hitchhiking. I think that in my four years at St. Ignatius, from 1950 to 1954, there may have been five times that I took a streetcar. I had to travel about eight miles to get to school, but we would hitchhike right down Ashland Avenue from the Southwest Side — most everybody was hitchhiking to get to school that way.

Sports were everything back then — that was the big thing. Sixteen-inch softball was huge, and there was very little hard ball being played. Everybody played in the "prairies," a common term for any vacant lot. And we played in the streets, including football, where you would dodge between the cars that were parked there.

It was nothing to say, "Go out for a pass, run around the third parked car, take a right and come back in." Games in the street were very common. Softball was often played at the corners of a block where you had the four sewer covers. Those were the bases and you played out in the center of the street.

Dating was sparse in high school — if there was any romance at all. You really went out with groups more than you did with any individual. I was a junior in high school when I went on my first date, and she was a next door neighbor across the gangway where I lived. My mother and her mother thought that it was okay, and that was how sophisticated it was or wasn't in the early 1950s. We went to her high school dance at Mercy High School, located on the Southwest Side, and then went out afterwards to the local malt shop, the Melody Mill, and then took the streetcar home. The girls pretty much kept to themselves during high school, and there were not a lot of activities between boys and girls in those days, unlike today.

Everybody was into rock and roll music in the mid-1950s, and there was always a dance on Sunday nights at St. Sabina at 78th and Racine. That was a very popular place, but there was a lot more standing around than there was dancing, with the boys on one end of the gym and the girls on the other. Those who were brave enough might ask somebody to dance, but normally the guys just stood with the other guys from the neighborhood or the high school that they attended together. So, there wasn't a lot of mixing even within the boy's groups, you pretty much stayed with your own.

There was a lot of smoking back in high school — an awful lot — everyone smoked. We had a "smoker" at St. Ignatius and when you opened the door to the room it looked like the whole world was on fire! How anybody could breathe in the smoker was beyond me — it just permeated the whole school with the smell of smoke! The room was reserved for seniors, but if you were really "cool" as a junior they might have let you in. Most all of the boys back then smoked, but a lot of the girls smoked, too. I don't recall anybody drinking either hard liquor or wine in high school, but there was a fair amount of beer being consumed.

We never went out to the suburbs in those days. You pretty much were still confined to the local neighborhood, or to the parish as it was called then. This continued to be the case into the mid-1950s, and even after television expanded our horizons. Now, you might have worked outside your neighborhood, but you didn't socialize too much outside your neighborhood. The jobs that I had in high school included, on Friday nights, loading the filler sections for the weekend editions of the *Chicago Tribune*. I would go down on the docks, and for $8.75 I loaded dozens and dozens of trucks with the big bundles of the filler that went out to the distributors for the Sunday papers.

Boys were expected to find some kind of job by the time they were into their teens. The main job, of course, was caddying, even though that meant a lot of hanging around. Virtually nobody in our age group played golf, because you just couldn't afford to. You could go out to a public course, like Pipe O' Peace on the Southeast Side. I laugh when I think of Tiger Woods hitting a golf ball 300 yards — you could hit the ball 300 yards at Pipe O' Peace because it was like concrete. They didn't have watered fairways, and the ball would go and go and go and you felt stronger than an ox.

I had the job with the *Tribune* on Friday nights, but I also had the luckiest job in the world — Andy Frain usher. I got that job just as I turned 15, in time for the national conventions of 1952. I was also an Andy Frain usher at the ballparks, the football games at Comiskey Park and Wrigley Field, the hockey games at Chicago Stadium, and the races at Arlington Park. Of course, you had to wear a uniform and white gloves and a hat as an usher, but it was the greatest job in the world for a kid. It paid $5 for a ball game and $6 for a doubleheader. You had to be there an hour and a half before game time and you had to stay, supposedly, an hour after the game, but seldom did anybody stay that long. You were also supposed to do crowd control, because that was a period when there was no security provided by the teams, and very few police were around the parks and stadiums.

My biggest fear as an usher was to be thrown off the second balcony of the Chicago Stadium during a hockey game! The crowd was rough — and there was nobody but fans up there. You were both the usher and security, but you were much more security than you were an usher. The hockey games were the toughest of all because they had the heaviest drinking, toughest guys, and they really did not like to be told to behave. We didn't have a walkie-talkie system, and there were no police up there, so we had no way to communicate any problems. I did that for three years, and it included summers as well as during the school year.

In 1952, the Republican Party held their national convention at the Amphitheater on Halsted. I was assigned to General Eisenhower's floor at the Blackstone Hotel during that convention. I was also the person who, following his nomination, was asked to open the door when he came down the corridor. Remember, I had just turned 15 years of age. I was standing there in the hall and somebody yelled, "He's coming, he's coming!" They had the television cameras in the corridor and the lights went on and I went to put the key in the door, but I couldn't get the key in the hole! So, General Eisenhower came down the corridor and said, "Young man, why don't you give me the key!" And he took the key and opened the door. It was my great claim to fame. He was very nice to me, but he could tell that I didn't know how to get a key in a door.

Looking back, the 1950s were really a quiet period for Americans — other than the Korean War. Jobs were available, friendships were strong, family was important and gas was cheap. You didn't have fancy dinners or do fancy things very often, but you really felt good about your lot in life. You never felt that the world owed you a living either. You really had to work for what you got, and I think that was an important lesson from that period as well.

There was still a sense of community that was very strong back then, too. People were willing to reach out and help. My whole life was characterized by a number of people who made a huge difference at various steps along the way, whether it was a nun in grade school or the principal of my high school. In every instance, somebody was there to be helpful. I don't believe that anybody is self-made. I believe that everybody receives some help along the way. That was a period where people did reach out. There were a lot of opportunities presented and a lot of people who were looking to be helpful, which I think is a great artifact of that period. We all worked hard and didn't ask much of others — but others did a great deal for us.

Jim O'Connor attended Holy Cross College and Harvard University. He recently retired as chairman of the board of Commonwealth Edison.

Northwest Side Stories | Jim Parker

I've spent most of my life on Chicago's Northwest Side. I was kind of a wild kid, so I've got some stories to tell. I grew up around Addison and Newland, and then we moved to Fletcher Street, right around Belmont and Pulaski. There were a lot of things to do in the neighborhood, like go to the Olsen Rug Garden, at Pulaski and Diversey — it was a wonderful place. It had a huge waterfall that cascaded down a tall hill. There were paths and walkways on the hill, with benches and seating so you could sit there and enjoy yourself. There were also ducks, sheep and farm animals for kids to go and see, as well. At night it was lit up with colored lights, and people would go there from all over the city, not just the neighborhood.

At Pulaski and Milwaukee was the Milford Theater, and we spent a lot of time there. On Saturday mornings you could watch 20 cartoons for $.25, and afterward they had the Duncan yo-yo contest — which I won once. Right next door to the theater was the Over-30 Dance, a dance hall for people over 30 years old. The name on the hall literally read, "Over-30 Dance." We used to always think, "My God, I'll never be over 30!" A little further north was the Buffalo Ice Cream Parlor, at Irving Park and Pulaski. They had a great soda fountain there, with fancy marble work and the old high back chairs to sit in. That was a place that attracted people from all over the city, too. Of course, if you went to a show at the Irving Theater, you'd always go across the street to the Buffalo for ice cream afterward.

When I was a little kid I got to go to Wrigley Field a lot. My mother worked there for about 20 years, and those were the days when your mother took you to work with her, so I'd be down there everyday. She ran the pop stand behind home plate, and my aunt and other family members worked there, too. My aunt made breakfast for all the big shots, like Joe "40,000" Murphy, who was head usher, and Tate, the pass gate usher. Murphy was a real character and he ran the place like a general. If something happened at the opposite end of the park he was there — I don't know how he'd get there so fast! He was loud, and you could hear him across the park giving orders.

I'd see all the behind the scenes stuff, like renting out the seat cushions, which kids could then pick up after the game in exchange for a free pass to the next day's game. I had the run of the ballpark — and got to meet a lot of the players. I used to sit with Cub's catcher Mickey Owen's kid sometimes. I even sat with Rogers Hornsby, who autographed a ball for me — years later my son took it outside to play pinners with! I've got dozens of balls that I had autographed. The players would always sign autographs on the way to the clubhouse before and after the games back then. I don't think they ever imagined their autographs would be worth so much today.

Back in those days the foul ball net behind home plate went up on an angle, all the way up to the grandstand. After a player hit a foul ball straight back, it would go up to the top, and slowly roll back down. Well, the whole crowd, everybody in unison, would make this sound — woooooooooooop — as the ball made its way down. I still talk to people today who remember that!

We lived around Addison and Newland, and I went to Lane Tech High School. Riverview Park was right behind the school, so I went over there to get a summer job. My first job there was working in the store room, passing out uniforms to the guys as they came to work from 7:00 to 11:00 in the morning. I then worked the Shoot-the-Chutes ride, which made me feel like a big shot, riding the boat down the slide. Every Tuesday we had ride test day, where we would go on the Bobs and the other roller coasters and stop them at the top. Then we had to get out and push — to test the brakes. At dinner time, we'd get a girl and go in the Mill and the Floss, which was the tunnel of love at the time, and float back in there for an hour.

I worked there for three years, and got to know how things worked pretty well. Remember the knockdown game? This was where you were supposed to knock down these dummies with a ball. Well, the guy always let you knock down the first one, but on the second toss, he would step on a board that moved up a little ledge that made it impossible for the knockdown to fall off. The "Strongman" sledgehammer game was also "rigged," and I worked that occasionally. I'd get these blowhards trying to impress their girlfriends, but when I'd turn this little tension screw there was no way in the world they were going to get the bell to ring. And you could make a guy a hero too — you could make a skinny, weak guy ring the bell by turning the screw the opposite way — it was fun! I'd work at Aladdin's Castle occasionally, where I'd blow the shot of air up the ladies' skirts — that was the "funnest" job I ever had in my life. For a kid to work in an amusement park it was great fun, and there was a real camaraderie at the park — like a family.

One summer I got a job working for Sam Leone down at Touhy Beach. Sam was a great guy, and a real character. Everybody loved him — he was like a saint. He had life made, with his own home right there on the beach. Of course, Sam loved to pull water skiers, and sometimes he would pull twenty water skiers at a time up and down the lakefront. I remember one time he was pulling me and

I was wearing an old bloomer-style bathing suit. I was doing okay for awhile, but when I got up around Evanston I went down and fell backwards in the water. Somehow I managed to pull myself back up, but my bathing suit was ripped and around my ankles. So, I'm yelling at Sam to stop, but he was notoriously hard of hearing — he was practically deaf — so I'm yelling and he can't hear a thing. Meanwhile, everybody up at the beach in Evanston is laughing and laughing!

Now, Sam believed in fiberglass, and he would always say, "Stronger than Steel!" So, he got this idea to build a fast, lightweight, fiberglass boat, which I helped him build. It would be a small, powerful boat that would take air in through the top of the gunnels, and then it let out underneath the boat. So, the faster the boat would go, the more it would lift up and out the water, and it would go even the faster — that was the principal at least. So, we worked on that thing all summer long and finally finished the boat — and then he let the lifeguards take it out. Well, just as soon as they took it out on the water and brought it up to speed the nose went up, the boat flipped over, and it sunk — just like that. What a sight it was! Poor Sam thought it was a great invention!

The lifeguards at Touhy Beach had all sorts of tricks they would play on the new recruits. A new guard would come in and they would tell him, "Go down to Loyola Beach and get 100 feet of shoreline." So, the kid would run down there and say, "Touhy Beach needs 100 feet of shoreline right now!" The guy there would say, "Well, geez, we're all out of shoreline. You got to go down to Ardmore!" These poor kids would be running down to Oak Street before they figured out it was a joke! Every lifeguard knew the joke, but not the new kids.

As I got older I got interested in politics. I saw Harry Truman march down Madison Street in a torchlight parade, and went to Kennedy's as well. When I got out of college I worked as a proof reader in the City Clerk's office. There were some colorful people working in politics back then. It was an amazing time to be at City Hall. I'd see Mayor Daley at meetings, and he used to have me run errands and deliver messages for him.

At Christmas one year I thought I'd get the mayor a gift. My father-in-law was Swedish, and he used to make this glug with raisins, spices and whiskey in a mason jar. Well, I was young, and I thought I would take this down to the mayor and give him some as a present. So, I went to his office and told his secretary, "I'd like to see the mayor." She asked if had an appointment, and I said no. But then she said, "Okay, Jim, go ahead in."

"What can I do for you?" the mayor asked.

"I brought you a jar of glug," I said, pulling out the mason jar from a brown paper bag, the raisins floating on top and the nuts spinning and bouncing around. He was overwhelmed, to say the least! When the mayor of Chicago asked what he could do for me I should have asked for a better job, not hand him some glug! I had no idea who I was with! But he was very nice about it, thanking me for doing a good job and giving me some advice.

I was a precinct captain back then, too, and I did a good job. In those days, when you needed something done in your neighborhood you called your precinct captain. If I couldn't get a city crew to fix a busted curb, I would get the cement and fix it myself. And I'd fix sidewalks and trim trees, too. These are the things you did to keep your precinct voting your way. I did some tricky stuff, too, like dumping a couch in an alley and then waiting for the call from a resident to come and pick it up for them. Then I'd go grab it, take credit for it as a favor done — and then dump it again in another alley! Most of the time I worked very hard, and many times I would get stiffed — like when a guy called to get help moving some stuff from his basement. I moved paper, bottles, and old junk all day long — and then a week later the guy puts his house up for sale! I'm doing all this work for the votes, and then he leaves the precinct!

But my job was to keep my three streets Democratic — Fletcher, Barry and Nelson — plus the 30 nuns at Madonna High School. And those nuns were solid — boom-boom-boom — they were always right there, first thing, on election day voting Democratic!

I remember one election day when a guy called me up and said, "Jim, you didn't drop off the beer and the whiskey."

I had just started the job and said, "What are you talking about?"

He says, "It's election morning — Joe (the previous precinct captain) always bought beer and whiskey."

"Well, how much do you need?" I said.

"A six pack of beer and a half pint," he says.

"You got to be kidding! For one vote?" I said.

"No — eight votes," he said.

"Eight votes," I said, "Don't move — I'll be right over!"

Jim Parker owned Copelin Commercial Photographers from 1967 until 2004, when he donated the studio's archive to the University of Illinois at Chicago. The collection contains over one million images, some dating to the mid-nineteenth century.

Summer Nights

"Mayor Daley Gets a Two-Base Hit," 1956
Photograph by Bill Quinn *Chicago Sun-Times*

Italian Street Festival at Chicago and Pulaski, 1953

Chicago Buddhist Church Carnival, 5487 S. Dorchester, c.1950
Photograph by James Numata
Japanese American Service Committee

Buddy Hackett at St. Michael's Church Carnival, 24th and Western, 1958

Kids at Riverview Park, 1950

Overnight Sleepers at North Avenue Beach, 1955

A 'Norman Rockwell' Childhood | Jim Thompson

I always thought I had a "Norman Rockwell" kind of childhood in my old neighborhood. I was born in 1936 and grew up in Garfield Park on Chicago's West Side. My father was going to medical school during those years, and then he started his own practice. I didn't want a medical career because I thought that my father worked too hard, so I went into law and politics instead, but I've had to work just as hard. His schedule was demanding, and he would often make house calls between 9 p.m. and Midnight — some of the these families couldn't pay for the visits. Then, on a lot of nights between Midnight and 2 a.m., he would do insurance exams for a few dollars. So, he worked really, really hard. Many times I would get out of school and travel with him during the night, sitting in the car while he did his exams. I would wait in the parked car, start the engine, turn the wheel, drive the car a little bit forward and backward. I thought that I was being really clever because I would always put the car back in the same place.

I went downtown by myself for the first time at ten years old, and I even dragged my younger brother with me. We just got on the Madison Street streetcar and rode it — we didn't know where we were going. So, we went downtown and wandered around, and took the streetcar back home. My parents didn't know that we were going to do that, and they were a little upset at the idea of a ten-year-old and six-year-old wandering around downtown by themselves. But those were different days. In fact, when I was thirteen my brother and I took an excursion out of Chicago on our own. My parents put us on a train to Niagara Falls, and we slept in our seats overnight. When we arrived they put us on a bus and took us to the Maid of the Mist ride. Then we walked around, got back on the train and returned to Chicago. It was just my brother and myself with a bunch of tourists — it was adventurous.

We used to play softball all the time when I was growing up, and we also used to play in in the abandoned factories in the area. We'd sneak in through broken windows and climb up and down the old machinery. We would walk along the railroad tracks and look for pieces of coal or put pennies on the rails. We'd also make cherry bombs and put them under tin cans and watch them explode. I have a lot of good memories of that time. I remember that after supper people would come out and sit on their front porches to watch their kids play in the street every night. I

had a Schwinn Roadmaster and would ride around the neighborhood on my bike. Although I didn't play much baseball in my early years, we would play pinners off the side of the buildings. Pinners was our favorite sport.

I was of the generation that grew up on radio, including the serials before dinner, and the shows like "Fibber McGee and Molly" after dinner. The whole family would listen to the after dinner radio shows, while my brother and I would listen to the serials. We got our first television set in 1949, a 13-inch black and white Admiral television — a little TV inside a big console. To get a clearer picture I took a piece of wire and attached it to the antenna leads and wrapped the other end around a coat hanger hung on the top of the drapes — and it worked. The first television shows that I remember included "The Texaco Theater with Milton Berle," and "Kukla Fran and Ollie" — I was a devoted watcher of that program.

I have always been interested in Chicago politics, and my memories go back to the Mayor Kennelly years — back when politics was an honorable thing to aspire and admit to. I had an early, early interest in politics and I always read the daily newspapers to keep up with things. We always read the papers at home, and I did a lot of reading by myself at libraries on a regular basis. Of course, we lived in an exciting ward, the 28th, and were part of the West Side bloc, so it was a very exciting thing to read about. I decided then to go to law school because I thought that it would be the quickest route into politics. Of course, after I graduated from law school and got my first job as a prosecutor, politics went on hold for 17 years. While I was in law school, I wanted to be a criminal defense lawyer. I thought that was wonderful, but my professor at Northwestern Law School persuaded me that I needed to start in the prosecutor's office to learn how things worked, then I could become a defense lawyer. So, I tried that and fell absolutely in love with it, and never did become a defense lawyer until later years.

I got hired by State's Attorney Benjamin Adamowski in his last year in office. Back then the office was intensely political. Luckily, I had a classmate who was a godson of Adamowski and the result of meeting him was that he took a liking to me. Adamowski and I became very close, and I was sworn in along with two other assistant state's attorneys. After I got hired, I did cases during the day and worked on

Adamowski's extraordinary mandamus cases after hours.

The 1960 elections were an interesting time. Everyone just assumed that Mayor Daley was working his heart out in Illinois to get Kennedy elected President, but local politics absolutely meant more to Richard J. Daley than national politics. I remember riding around on election day in Alderman Vito Marzullo's ward. I was in the squad car with the policemen and we passed one of these polling places with plate glass windows down to the basement — and there were four legs in one of the polling booths. I raced in and went over to the booth and started to complain. One of polling judges came over to me and said that the "boss" wanted to see me. I said, "Who's the boss?"

"Alderman Marzullo," he said.

"I don't work for him," I said. "I work for the State's Attorney."

The judge insisted I see Marzullo, so I went over to see him. He said, "Young man, what are you doing in my ward?"

I said, "I'm doing poll watching and I'm finding four-legged voters."

He said, "Kid, we don't need some outsiders in this ward. Now, you just go someplace else for the rest of the day!" Which, of course, I ignored and kept touring his ward.

Years later, when I was governor of Illinois, I always had an affection for the West Side political bosses. I used to call up Marzullo and say, "I need a vote on this bill from your guys, both Democrats and Republicans." I could always get Vito to call the state representatives and get those votes. Then, in 1979, Pope John Paul II was visiting Chicago and I was at the airport — as governor. The Pope left his plane and the nuns raced up to him, and I saw Vito at the airport looking around. I said to Vito, "What are you doing here?"

He said, "I want to meet the Pope."

I said, "Well, you come with me." I grabbed his hand and dragged him over and forced our way through the crowd to the Pope. Now, I didn't know the protocol, so I just said, "Pope, this is Vito. Vito, this is the Pope." And, Vito was just thrilled beyond words to meet the Pope on the airport tarmac.

James Thompson served four-terms as governor of Illinois. He is currently chairman of the Winston and Strawn law firm.

Boaters at Garfield Park, c.1950
Chicago Public Library Special Collections

The 'Perfect Place' | Bob Polster

Albany Park was a great place to grow up during the 1950s, and I remember it as being a perfect place. Kids fended for themselves and didn't need parents to structure their activities or drive them around. The main thing I remember is the sense of freedom we had, there was no reason to be paranoid in the 1940s or 1950s. You were safe and you could explore your neighborhood without fear.

In those years, if you wanted to go to the park or play, you could do it without depending upon your parents. Even at the age of 10 or 11, I could leave my house in the morning, say goodbye to my mother, and go and play. Of course, I'd come home for lunch, but then I'd go out for the rest of the afternoon. There was unlimited playtime with an unlimited number of kids to do an unlimited number of activities. Even though I had no money, it wouldn't cost me anything to play lineball, pinners, or lag pennies. You wouldn't need any money, and you wouldn't need any help from your parents. Nowadays, everything is parent-related and parent-connected. It was great to grow up in those days, and I wouldn't have wanted to grow up in any other way.

We used to spend a lot of time playing at the Volta school yard. That was probably the main attraction for me and my neighborhood friends, and I went there more than any other place in my old neighborhood. There was also a gravel field across the street from my grammar school that was part of the grounds. So, we constantly went to the school and played lineball there, as well as pinners and fast pitching. We also played lineball in the streets, and it didn't matter if there were cars parked there or not. In Albany Park, everything was accessible, and it would only take five minutes to walk to any place we wanted to play.

In 1959, my family moved to Skokie, as many people from Albany Park did. They picked Skokie because of the strong Jewish identity and concentration. It was also because, for the first time, they could afford to buy a house — $28,000. They never could own before and it had always been their dream. For me, however, nothing in the suburbs could replace the combination of the school yard and playing in the streets and alleys.

Our house was constructed by Zale Builders on Crawford Avenue. My street was made up of houses that had been built either by Zale or Sears Builders — Sears was a big builder in my area. A section on the east side of Crawford, between Dempster and Church, was called Sears Electronic Homes. The sudden boom in my section of Skokie began in the mid-1950s — peo-ple had more money by then. Skokie changed dramatically in the 1950s — within just a few years all the streets were built and the housing developments went up — just like that.

After we moved to Skokie, I started my second year of high school at Niles West, a school for freshmen and sophomores. Niles East had just been built and was used for juniors and seniors only. The teachers in the Skokie schools were really different than the ones in the city. They were young, they were innovative, and weren't stagnant in their teaching methods. And they would do different things from day-to-day in their classrooms. They also had equipment available to them in the suburban schools that was not provided in classrooms in the Chicago Public Schools.

So, the difference between the schools in the city and the suburbs was big — like going from high school to college. I was getting good grades at Roosevelt High School by trying a little bit, but I had to work much harder to get a "C" at Niles than I did to get an "A" at Roosevelt. The caliber was almost college-level, and the teachers expected you to do all your homework — and everybody did it. I had to work a lot harder, and all my friends would study all the time for the tests. The suburban kids took things much more seriously than we ever did at Roosevelt. Many of my friends who didn't move from the old neighborhood and then went to college were overwhelmed by the work load.

As I remember it, the kids who lived in the suburbs were a bit more spoiled than city kids, especially the ones who had lived in the suburbs for a long time. They always had more money, and they wouldn't walk or ride their bikes as far — it just seemed like they were used to having everything. A lot of kids were snobbish in high school, especially the girls who had been in Skokie longer and had more money. So, I felt much more comfortable dating girls from Chicago. Luckily, there were many kids in my school who had just moved to the suburbs, so we were all in the same situation, and many became my friends. The kids from the city had a lot in common, so it didn't take long to make new friends.

For fun we went to movies at the Old Orchard Theater, Teatro del Lago or the Glencoe Theater. The only drive-in I remember going to was the Sunset Drive-In on McCormick between Touhy and Howard. I also played miniature golf around there at the little course in Lincolnwood near Lincoln Village. I also bowled a lot during the '50s, usually at the Twin Orchards Bowl on Skokie Boulevard. We rarely went downtown when I

lived in Skokie, but we dated girls from Chicago, so we made it to the city a lot. Sometimes we went to It's Here in Chicago, a coffee house near the Granada Theater, or a group of us would go for pizza at Papa Milano's or other places near Peterson and California. By the time we were juniors and seniors, girls in Skokie would be looking for college guys, so we would date younger girls who lived in Chicago and attended north side high schools like Mather, Sullivan and Von Steuben. We had socials and dances with BBG groups from Chicago, and it was a great way for us to meet girls.

One interesting difference between kids in the city and Skokie was that, in Chicago, groups of guys would always be doing things together: playing cards, hanging out at the beach, or congregating in one place to play sports. In the suburbs, it was very rare for there to be a large group of guys together. Kids usually didn't hang out in large groups at the parks or outside — maybe just three or four people. In Albany Park, I had many friends who lived close to each other — you might know twenty guys who lived within a few blocks of your house or apartment. To know twenty guys in the suburbs you would have to go miles and miles. So, people simply weren't as accessible in Skokie as they were in the city.

In the suburbs, kids seemed to have much more idle time on their hands — sometimes getting into trouble or doing pranks. The sense of "neighborhood" was com-

pletely different in the suburbs. In Chicago, you generally knew the people in your apartment building or on your block, but in the suburbs, your sense of closeness extended only to the nearby houses. And you had so much more going on in the city in such a small area. Even if something wasn't close you always could get on a bus, whereas bus service in the suburbs was very sketchy. I remember having to wait an hour for a bus in Skokie, while it was only a ten minute wait in Chicago. And you might have to walk a great distance just to get to a bus stop in the suburbs.

Looking back on the 1950s, I think that what made it so special was the feeling of innocence — kids didn't worry about the future or the world. Despite the threats from abroad, we didn't worry about tomorrow — the world was going to be there. It just seemed to be worry-free. We didn't have a fear of people, or pretty much anything during those years. And there seemed to be an unlimited potential to do anything we wanted to do as we grew up. It didn't even occur to us that we might not be able to do what we wanted to — or become who we wanted to be.

Bob Polster attended the University of Wisconsin before starting a career in education.

Above: *Mister Softee Ice Cream Man, North Side, c.1958*

Hungry?

Tell Lunch, 129 N. Union, c.1950
Eric Bronsky Collection

Candy Store, 530 N. Carpenter, c.1950
Eric Bronsky Collection

Lou's Restaurant, 1206 E. 63rd Street, c.1950
Photograph by Rubin Goldman

"Leras Grand Opening," Woodlawn, c.1950
Photograph by Rubin Goldman

Hot Dog Wagon, North and Homan, 1954

Farwell Pharmacy, Farwell and Clark, c.1950

Neighborhood Crime 101 | Jerry Petacque

Here is a thumbnail sketch of the hierarchy of the Chicago Police Department: first, it was called the "bureau" back then, and the police elite of Chicago were located at 11th and State — it was a police department within the police department. In the building they had the various bureaus, including a robbery detail, a confidence and bank detail, bomb and arson detail, robbery detail and homicide detail. Each one of these details had a lieutenant in charge of that particular bureau. They would all wear big-brimmed hats and suits — not uniforms. They were considered the elite of the police department, and the bureau was separate from the police. These guys felt that they had all the intellect and ability to solve any big crime that took place in the City of Chicago, while the regular police department was expected to solve domestic crimes and cases of less significance. This was the heart of the crime bureau in Chicago, and they also worked in liaison with the FBI and other federal authorities. My father, Ralph David Petacque, was a lieutenant on the police force, and, at first, he was head of the confidence detail.

A good example of his work on this detail were guys who preyed on wealthy widows. Back in those days they had a number of dance studios in the Chicago area. So, one 80 year-old widow from Lake Forest, who had an inheritance of $20 million, wanted dance lessons. She went to a Chicago dance studio and wound up with a $500,000 contract for dance lessons, because they had a young, intelligent, good-looking gigolo-type instructor who ingratiated her and got her to sign a huge contract. In another case, there was a guy who preyed on wealthy and religious women. He would start dating these women because they were lonely, and he would usually meet them in church because they were very religious. Eventually, he would develop a relationship with these women, then he would say to a typical victim, "I have a vision. You have to get naked and hold a crucifix above you. I will then take your picture, because I have a vision that this is what you should do." So, of course, the naïve, very lonely, very religious lady would pose for the picture. Once he had the picture, he would call the lady back and say, "Look, Mrs. X, I have a photo of you in the nude. Do you want me to tell your family about this picture?" So, he would extort money from these poor, lonely, very wealthy religious ladies. My father caught this criminal, and he was named "The Crucifix Con Man."

My father made some major arrests during that period, and eventually, he became a police captain. An important case for my father was the one known as the "Nun Rapist Case." In the early 1950s, there were a number of rapes of nuns by an unknown assailant. Since my father was very close to Cardinal Stritch at that time, he received a call from him, who said, "Dave, we have a major problem. We don't want to go to the newspapers on this issue because the nuns are sworn to celibacy. If they are raped, it is very traumatic in terms of their celibacy vow to God. So, it cannot be reported in the newspapers." So, my father interviewed a number of the nuns and they gave a description of a young person. One of the nuns told my dad that this kid said, "You'll never catch me because I'm a runaway." My dad began to do research on runaway kids. Apparently there was a kid in Chicago who was a runaway, and my dad interviewed his parents who said their son was in California in the Los Angeles area. My father called the police in California and they picked up the kid. He then confessed in California, and my father went all the way there by train to pick up the kid and bring him back to Chicago. The cardinal and the church were very grateful to my father for solving the case, and the kid was convicted.

During that era, a lot of stolen goods from department stores would wind up with fences who would move the goods. There was a very famous fence in Chicago named "Fish" Johnson, and he knew my father. Fish was a nice, outgoing person who would hang around restaurants on the Northwest Side. The problem for my father was that a lot of wealthy people, including some politicians, would go to Fish to get their "K-Mart discount" on stolen goods. So, even though my father knew what Fish was doing, he left him alone — until my father became head of the robbery and burglary detail — then Fish came under his purview at the bureau. Fish had a place on Armitage that had a huge inventory, and, eventually, his business got so large and he became so brazen that he had to be shut down. When his operation was finally closed, there was a newspaper article that appeared with the headline, "The Fish Has Been Taken Out of the Pond."

Jerry Petacque, attorney, artist and writer, is the brother of the late Art Petacque, crime reporter for the Chicago Sun-Times.

Neighborhood Politics 101 | Richard Elrod

In 1955, I was a senior at Northwestern University. It was a mayoral election year, and for a political science course I chose to write a paper examining the races in two city wards. First, I chose the 44th Ward, because they had both strong Republican and Democratic organizations. Second, I chose the 24th Ward, because they had a very strong ward organization and my father was the committeeman.

There were three people running in the Democratic primary for mayor that year: Richard J. Daley, who was the County Clerk and the County Chairman of the Democratic party; Martin Kennelly, who was the incumbent Mayor for two terms; and Frank Keenan, who was the County Assessor and also the committeeman for the 49th Ward.

After the polls closed, we went to my father's office in the 24th Ward. He was sitting behind a desk and taking the returns from the precinct captains. As they would come in they would hand my father their returns, and tell him what the results were, saying, "Daley-502, Kennelly-5 and Keenan-2." My father would say, "Great work, you did a heck of a job!" Then, another captain would come in, saying "Daley-420 and Keenan-12." This continued throughout the night, and as the results came in I was looking to see where the precincts were and how the demography and socio-economics affected the votes. Then, an unusual precinct came in: Daley-32 and Keenan-480.

I said, "Dad, that's right next to a precinct that came in big for Daley." He said, "Oh, that's Izzy's precinct. He works in the assessor's office, so he had to have his precinct come in big for Keenan." I was just amazed at the influence the precinct captains had over their voters.

In those days, on election night, the committeemen would have to come downtown to the Morrison Hotel and report their returns to Daley. When you have great election returns, you are very braggadocio about it — you wanted the party leaders to see them and hopefully would be rewarded for your work. As a matter of fact, after the 1948 election, my father received tickets to President Truman's inauguration in Washington, D.C.. Once there, he wanted to go up to congratulate the president, but, naturally, the security stopped him because he didn't have the credentials. My father pulled out his ward returns as a committeeman — something like 20,000 votes for Truman and 300 votes for Dewey, and said, "Give this to the president, and I think that these numbers will be good enough credentials." After a minute, the guard said, "The president will see you now."

During that 1948 campaign, I went to Philadelphia with my father for the Democratic National Convention. That was the year the Dixiecrats, led by Richard Russell and Strom Thurmond, walked out, and Hubert Humphrey, then the mayor of Minneapolis, gave the keynote address — he was just fantastic. This was also the year Colonel Jacob Arvey, who was a powerful Democratic National Committeeman, put out some overtures to General Dwight D. Eisenhower to run for president as a Democrat. Truman heard about it and was, naturally, very upset that someone was trying to undercut his candidacy. Many Democrats, however, didn't think that Truman was electable in 1948. After Eisenhower turned them down, the Democratic Party of Illinois was very strong for Truman.

During the 1960 election I was a precinct captain in the 50th Ward. Of course, John F. Kennedy, the Democratic presidential candidate, was Catholic, and I had some very staunch Republicans living in my precinct who also happened to be Catholic. So, the week before the election I went around my precinct putting Kennedy pictures in everyone's windows. Of course, I didn't stop at any Republican's homes, but a man came out and said, "Hey, Elrod, why are you skipping me?" I said, "I didn't think that you wanted a Democrat in your window." He said, "Well, it's Kennedy, so naturally I will." His Catholicism came out more strongly than his political preferences, and Kennedy carried my precinct heavily.

I still remember representing the 50th Ward in the big Kennedy torch light parade that year. It started in Grant Park and then headed west, all the way to the Chicago Stadium. Each ward was responsible for bringing a certain amount of people to the parade — if you had to bring 300 people, then 100 people would march in the parade, 100 people would line Madison Street, and 100 got to go into the stadium. Since we were in the 50th Ward, we were the last to kickoff, because they went from 1 through 50. We spent a great deal of money and time building a float for that parade, but by the time our ward finally got close to the stadium Kennedy had already been there, spoken and was on his way to the airport — just as we were arriving for the big event!

Richard Elrod, attorney and Cook County Circuit Court judge, was Cook County sheriff for 16 years.

The Streetcar's Demise | Jeff Wien

I started riding the buses and streetcars in Chicago at the age of ten, which by today's standards is totally unheard of. In the early 1950s, my parents didn't have any fear for their young children going off alone. In fact, I used to get on the Evanston "L" in north Evanston and ride to Howard Street and then on to downtown Chicago. I used to ride to the Merchandise Mart on Saturday mornings to attend live WMAQ radio shows for kids. One show was "Uncle Ned's Squadron," which I appeared on several occasions. I would also visit friends on the North Side, taking the "L" to Wilson where I would transfer to a Broadway streetcar — all at the ages of 10 and 11. It was an era of innocence back then. Believe it or not, I went to the 1952 Republican Convention at the International Amphitheater alone. I took the "L" to 40th and Indiana and then the Stockyards "L" over to the Amphitheater. I was down on the floor carrying banners at 11 years old! I guess it's pretty amazing my parents would let me do that.

I became very familiar with the transit system at an early age, and felt comfortable going anywhere. I loved to stand up front in the streetcar with the motorman — with the wind blowing in my face — it was so much fun. You had this big, massive vehicle rolling down the middle of the street, with the noise of the traction motors grinding, the air compressor going "thump-thump-thump," and the sound of the air brakes and doors operating. I really liked them! I once rode the entire length of the Western Avenue streetcar, from 79th Street on the South Side to Berwyn Avenue on the North Side, for the simple pleasure of it.

In 1956, while trying to ride that very Western Avenue streetcar to Riverview Park, I learned that they had been replaced on that route by propane buses the previous Sunday. When I got on the bus I asked the driver, "Where are the streetcars?" He said, "They're gone — they do not run here anymore." I was stunned. I also learned of other routes where streetcars were slated for replacement. It was then that I realized that the days for the Chicago streetcars were indeed numbered, and I would do my best to photograph the remaining ones. I purchased an 8 mm Bell & Howell movie camera and immediately started the work. Taking the movies was no easy task, because I was still in high school at the time, and streetcars only operated on weekdays. Whenever I had a free moment after school I would travel from Evanston to film the streetcars on the North Side of Chicago. People would come up to me and

say, "What are you doing? You're filming the streetcars? Who cares? You are crazy! Good riddance to them!" By the end of the summer of 1957 I had very good film coverage of Clark Street, which was fortunate, because on September 7th the CTA operated the last streetcar on Clark between Howard Street and the Loop.

In early 1958, it was announced by the CTA that the last streetcar run in Chicago was scheduled to operate on Wentworth Avenue the morning of June 21, 1958. About a week or so before the run I asked a CTA employee, "Why aren't you having some kind event honoring the last run?" He said, "That's the end of an era — something we'd like to forget." They gave no publicity to it at all. There was no nostalgia in those days, they wanted to modernize everything. This was a mindset of the 1950s, and historic preservation of any sort was not important in those days.

Our society in the 1950s became more and more automobile-oriented, and it seemed the goal was to get all the streetcars out of the city as fast as possible. The "Green Hornet" streetcars only ran for ten years, from 1948 to 1958, yet similar cars are still running in San Francisco. There was no will to keep the operation going here, despite their benefits, particularly the ecological ones.

When I look at my movies now I can't help but notice how efficiently the traffic moved. The amount of traffic is so small compared to today. The streets looked abandoned during the 1950s, when many more people were using public transportation instead of driving their own cars.

On that fateful day of the final streetcar run, I left my Evanston home around Midnight. I took the "L" to the Loop where I boarded streetcar #7213 at 2:30 a.m. I squeezed on board with about 100 other rail fans and rode up and down Wentworth Avenue during the rest of the night and early morning hours. Nobody talked really, we all just absorbed the experience. When we arrived at the CTA's car barn at 78th and Vincennes Avenue everyone was ordered off the car. The doors closed, the conductor rang his bell to the motorman for the last time, the motorman rang his trolley gong for the last time, and the last streetcar pulled into the barn at 6:00 a.m., ending 99 years of streetcar service in Chicago.

Jeff Wien is a transit historian who is currently president of the Central Electric Railfans' Association.

The Drive-In's Rise | Maurie Berman

I was born in Albany Park and graduated from Von Stueben High School in 1943. I went into the Service after I turned 18, and, after two-and-half years, enrolled in business school on the GI Bill. I was selling hardware on the side to make a living and going to school at night. Schools were bursting with students back then because of the GI Bill, and anything calling itself a school was flooded with students.

You see, after the war GIs started coming back home. Their careers and lives were interrupted — they were in a state of bewilderment. A lot of them were gravitating towards two jobs. First, GIs were buying old cars — they had to be old because they weren't making them in between 1942 and 1945 — painting them a gaudy color and becoming taxi drivers. Second, a number of GIs were buying abandoned streetcar bodies or over-the-road tractor bodies, cutting a hole in them for a window, and becoming a hot dog seller. The city was just replete with these hot dog operations. My wife, Flory, and I, being hot dog aficionados, would go out several evenings a week sampling the different vendors. Not too many had a product they could be proud of.

Well, one night in January 1948, while being unable to sleep, I kept thinking: what could I do over the summer so that my winter would be free for studying for my CPA? I decided I was going to sell hot dogs, and do a better job than these other guys with their push carts, trailers and converted streetcars — and it would be a drive-in. I wrote down all my plans on accounting pads that night: how many days a week we'd be open and so on. And the name would be Superdawg. Superman had just become a popular figure, and everything was super-this and super-that. I remember writing to King Features Syndicate in New York because Superman was a trademark name and I didn't want to infringe on the copyright. I never got an answer — so what the heck — let's call it Superdawg! I didn't want to call it Maurie's Hot Dogs because the business was only going to be a short term venture. I wanted to pick a name that would have a life after I went into practice and sold the place.

The location we chose was really remote at that time. Who ever goes to Milwaukee and Devon? Most of the neighborhood residences weren't built back then. Niles was north of here, and Des Plaines was west of here, and there was no pedestrian traffic. I liked the location because of the proximity to the forest preserve and Whalen Pool, which drew lots of people on the weekends for picnics. Unfortunately, it would take us a while to figure out that people usually bring their own food to picnics.

Two weeks before we opened, the famous paper mache figures of Maurie and Flaurie were atop the building. Then, in May of 1948, with the grand investment of $6000, which was wedding present money, Superdawg opened. We ran from spring until Halloween, and during the winter months I went to school.

In May of 1950 I passed the CPA exam, so the purpose for which the business was being run had ended. But the business had really begun to take hold. In that first season we did $20,000, and I thought we were on our way. With borrowed money, we decided to exercise the option to buy the rented property we were operating on.

Until 1951, we had used only high school and college kids for help, which we found impractical because they were always going to dances and school activities. So, we began using adults. But it was difficult for our employees financially to only operate six months a year. We decided to try and operate year-round, so we could retain our people. To some this seemed foolish. Chicago is too cold! How do you stand it up there? People don't go out in winter! But we were aware that when it got cold, people didn't hibernate. They put a coat on, and went out. That is what happened, and our business was moderately profitable during the winter.

There were a lot of drive-ins back then. In this area, there was Henry's Drive-in, Topper's, Richard's Drive-in, Tastee Freeze, A&W and Dog 'N' Suds. Then, after McDonald's opened in Des Plaines in 1955, there were 1000s of imitators — and I mean 1000s — but only a few remain today. Remember, when McDonald's first opened there was no inside service or dining area — that came later. And once they began their self-service operation they eliminated the need for additional personnel — people became their own servers and carhops.

Most of these other drive-ins were primarily ice cream places. We served food, and we always worked hard to make the best possible hot dog. During the infrequent vacations we had, it wasn't where we were going to have dinner that night, it was where we were going to have hot dogs that night. We tried to sample the product any place we visited. Eventually, we found a company to produce our own formula for hot dogs. A Superdawg is an all-beef hot dog, mustard, our neon green relish, pure white onions, a pickled green tomato and a Kosher dill pickle — and we don't package it like an old fish! We wanted to give the customer a better product, better produced, presented better — and, of course, car service!

Maurie Berman's Superdawg Drive-In was recently included in the book 1000 Places to See Before You Die.

The Women of Austin

Taken around 1950, these photographs are part of a series that document life in the Austin neighborhood on Chicago's West Side. While it is unknown why the photographer originally chose to take these street portaits, today they offer a glimpse of city life at mid-twentieth century.

2 LET'S GO DOWNTOWN

The Loop was thriving in the 1950s. Thousands of residents, suburbanites and tourists flooded downtown Chicago to shop and be entertained — in addition to those who commuted and worked there regularly. During the day, there was a palpable energy on the streets as businessmen rushed to their offices, newspaper vendors hawked the city's four dailies and shoppers moved from store to store. At night, the Loop was still abuzz as singles met for drinks in the clubs, hungry diners filled the restaurants, and theater crowds mingled under the brightly-lit marquees on Randolph and State Streets. Chicago was the most exciting American city east of New York in those years, and for those lucky enough to have experienced it, the memories are still strong today.

The Crossroads of America

Chicago was considered the crossroads of the continent during the 1950s because it served as the nerve center of America's railway system — the dominant means of travel at the time. Nineteen different rail lines and numerous other connecting belt railroads brought hundreds of trains and thousands of passengers to the city daily, filling the six Loop depots with commuters and tourists.

For those taking trains cross-country, Chicago was a natural place to spend a few hours shopping or sightseeing while waiting for a connecting train. Unlike O'Hare Airport today, the Loop's train stations were within close proximity to the city's favorite destinations, most within walking distance. Many long-distance travelers chose to spend a night in Chicago, perhaps enjoying a meal and stage show before continuing their journey the next day.

The city's geographical location also made it a natural choice to hold conventions and expositions, with regular events being held in the Loop's largest hotels, like the Conrad Hilton, Palmer House and Pick Congress, and the city's show halls, like the Chicago Coliseum, International Amphitheater and the Chicago Stadium. This steady stream of conventioneers kept the Loop's restaurants and clubs filled, as well as the city's many burlesque venues, which catered to the out-of-town crowd. Free entertainment guides advertising these bawdy clubs could be found in hotels and tourist attractions, most promising cheap drinks, loud music and skimpy outfits on the showgirls.

Tourism in general was big business in those years, with sightseers coming from around the Midwest just to take in the "big city" feel. For families, particularly those from flat, rural states, the city's impressive architecture and skyline were worth the trip alone. Chicago's skyscrapers, small by today's standards, were a popular destination, including observation decks in the Wrigley Building, Board of Trade and the Prudential Building, which after its completion in 1955 was the city's tallest building at 41 stories. The vistas of the city looked markedly different back then — instead of the modern glass and steel we see today it was a brick and mortar town, with very little color compared to Chicago of the twenty-first century. At times the city could even have a dark, foreboding appearance due to nearly a century of coal-burning furnaces and engines, which further darkened the appearance of the Loop's monotone buildings.

Loop Shopping

Before Chicago had shopping malls there was State Street, and when combined with the rest of the Loop's specialty shops and boutiques it made the city a world-class destination for finding just about anything. State Street was in its prime in the 1950s, and all the big department stores were still there — Marshall Field's, Carson Pirie Scott, the Fair Store, Goldblatt's, Mandel Brothers and Sears — each with its own personality and inspiring its own strong loyalties. In addition, hundreds of smaller specialty shops lined the street, from confectionary treats at Demet's to women's wear at Charles A. Stevens. All of the city's neighborhoods had their own shopping districts, many with large department stores, but nothing could compare with the selection and class of State Street's finest stores.

Shopping in the Loop was considered a special occasion in those years, and proper attire was worn by all, including children, who would be required by parents to wear their own "best" clothes. Men wore jackets, ties and fedoras — and a sea of crisp, perfectly blocked hats could always be seen moving through the Loop. Ladies wore only dresses and skirts — pants were practically unheard of for women in those years. Rules of etiquette were always respected at the better department stores, like Marshall Field's, where white-gloved operators worked the elevators and the third floor waiting room was nationally known for its style and elegance.

Beyond State Street, a fascinating array of shops and businesses could be found in the Loop, from "Jewelers Row" on Wabash Avenue to the specialty music shops in the Fine Arts Building. Little stores with esoteric interests could be found everywhere, from the upper floors of dingy office buildings to the lobbies of hotels. It was a city where almost anything could be found and purchased, with much redundancy, yet a city of favorites — favorite newsstands, candy stores, book dealers and tobacco shops.

For children and teenagers, the Loop offered a world of kid-friendly stores, including magic shops, toy departments, and hobby shops — and kids often shopped on their own. In fact, it was not uncommon for children, some as young as eight or nine years old, to travel downtown alone to see a dentist or doctor, then go to a favorite store, movie or simply walk around the Loop in awe of the surroundings.

Of course, going downtown during the holidays was a ritual for most Chicagoans, children and adults alike. The annual Christmas parade was a fixture in the 1950s, with brightly colored holiday characters lining the route as floats made their way down State Street. Fanciful holiday window displays were also a prime attraction for shoppers, the most elaborate created by Marshall Field's, which spent much of the year designing, constructing and decorating their vignettes. The Christmas windows, along with dining under the enormous tree in the Walnut Room, made Field's the dominant retailer during the holiday season.

Downtown Restaurants

A good meal was part of any downtown visit, whether it be a quick bite at a cafeteria or a full dinner in an elegant dining room. The Loop was filled with hundreds of possibilities: restaurants, steakhouses and coffee shops served American, Chinese and German food in office buildings, hotels or even On Top of the Rock, the Prudential Building's observatory-level dining room.

This was the era before healthy eating became part of the popular culture, so menus were laden with heavy, beef-oriented dishes and entrees. Menus were much bigger in the '50s compared to today (they were literally larger in size as well), offering a wide range of selections, though vegetarians would have been hard-pressed to find anything to order at many eateries. "Old World" cuisine and attitude ruled, with the emphasis on taste and experience over speed and calorie-counting.

Great food served in the Chicago tradition could be found at Henrici's, the Berghoff and Fritzel's, but theme-oriented restaurants were also becoming popular, including fancifully-decorated Polynesian, Italian and Swedish eateries. It was also popular to link dinner and entertainment in one location, like watching an ice stage production at the Boulevard Room, listening to music at the Blackhawk Restaurant or dancing at the Mayfair Room of the Blackstone Hotel.

For many Chicagoans, dining in the Loop's best restaurants was saved only for special occasions, like marking an anniversary, birthday or school prom. For these events, many restaurants employed photographers who went table-to-table taking pictures of couples and groups and then sold them as souvenirs. It was also popular for patrons to take home matchbooks, ashtrays, menus and even silverware as mementos.

With thousands of people working downtown, lunch crowds were always enormous. Workers packed their favorite restaurants daily, as well as the many cafeterias and lunch counters, which also offered good food but with a smaller menu selection. Wabash Avenue, in particular, had many small lunch spots to choose from, including those located in the office buildings that lined the street. National fast food chains, which dominate the Loop today, had yet to arrive, but there were plenty of hamburger shops, like White Palace and Wimpy's, the "home of the glorified hamburger."

'The Toddlin' Town'

During the 1950s, Chicago's Loop was nationally known for its entertainment circuit, and with movie theaters, jazz venues and burlesque clubs, there was something for everybody. The biggest stars played Chicago, and thousands of adoring fans came out every night to see them.

For most of the decade the Loop's movie palaces were enormously popular, and with over 15 theaters showing movies, stage shows and theatrical productions, the theater district was a hub of activity. These were the days of seeing live acts on stage before and after the movies, including performers like Bob Hope, Dean Martin and Jerry Lewis, Ella Fitzgerald and Cab Calloway. Capacities for some of these theaters were enormous: 2400 at the Palace Theater, 2600 at the State Lake Theater, 3200 at the Oriental and the biggest of all Loop theaters — the Chicago — at 3869. Long lines of patrons snaked around the block in front of theaters, and with crowds this size the laughs seemed bigger and the applause seemed louder. Before the popularity of television, movies were the primary form of entertainment, so crowds were large and very enthusiastic — making the experience of seeing a movie quite different from today.

The city's music and dance clubs were also well-attended in the '50s, with the Chez Paree being the most popular of all. Many couples celebrated their anniversaries to the sounds of the great performers who played there, including Sammy Davis Jr., Louis Prima, and Nat "King" Cole. The Mayfair Room, the Lotus Room and the Glass Hat continued to offer music and dancing, just as they did during the war years when thousands consistently filled the clubs.

By the early 1960s, however, downtown entertainment venues began to lose their appeal as newer and "hipper" entertainment spots were opening in other parts of the city, particularly on the Near North Side. The success of these clubs, coupled with the popularity of television, left Chicago's Loop searching for a new identity. Politicians wanted to see change too, and an "out with the old" attitude brought many of the Loop's most cherished and historically significant structures down, beginning a move towards the modern and new. Change would be quick — and painful — as the wrecking ball took down building after building.

The Loop seemed to have room for everybody in its best years — Minsky's Burlesque operated down the street from the stately Chicago Theater, while the arcades, tattoo parlors and flop houses of the south Loop never seemed to threaten shoppers to the north. Eventually, a new Loop would emerge, but in the 1950s the old Loop, even with a little dirt and rough edges, was a place to remember.

Page 70: *State Street, 1954*
CTA Photograph Collection

Spires and Skyscrapers

Panorama of the Loop From One North Lasalle Building, 1955

Sunshine and Shadow

"Chicago River on a Foggy Day," 1955
Photograph by Bill Sturm *Chicago Sun-Times*

Chicago Public Library, Washington Street Entrance , c.1955
Under the Chicago Theatre Marquee, c.1955

Shoppers on Washington, c.1955

Under the "L" Tracks on Wabash, c.1955

Looking North on Michigan, c.1955

Loop Alley, c.1955

Looking West on Madison From the "L" Platform, c.1955

Looking North on Wabash, c.1955

A Rainy Night on Madison, c.1955

Under the Lindbergh Beacon, c.1959

'The Loop Was Alive' | Bill Gleason

When I came back from World War II, I was in the Loop almost every day. In the late '40s and early '50s the Loop was the mecca — the Loop was alive — even after Midnight. People would come out of the hotels, particularly in the nice weather, because air conditioning wasn't a big thing yet, and socialize. Men would be outside talking about baseball, horse races, politics — anything that you can imagine.

I was so excited about being in the Loop. The skyline wasn't as magnificent as it is now, but it was still great and gave you such pride in the city. Chicago is one of the few great cities of the world. When I was a kid, there were 4,000,000 living in the city, but so many have moved out to the suburbs.

In the '50s, the Loop was really a fairyland, and I loved to wander in and out of Marshall Field's and Carson's — I was always a big Carson's fan. Then, I would go south on State to Goldblatt's, where we could find tremendous bargains. All of the big department stores were downtown, including Wieboldt's and Sears. If you weren't represented in the Loop, you might as well get out of the business. I remember the lavishness of Marshall Field's and the beauty of the women who worked there — that was also true of Carson Pirie Scott. I also remember the elevator operators at Field's because they wore white gloves. I remember the elevator operators everywhere, because every building had them. I also remember the omnipresent noise of the "L" and the things that might fall on you from the elevated trains and tracks, like pigeon droppings.

It was a just a delightful decade for us South Siders. It was the decade of the White Sox. After 30 years in the shadows, the Sox emerged and took back the town from the Cubs.

From 1950 through 1959, the Cubs drew a million paying customers in just two seasons. This was the franchise that went over a million in attendance five times in the second half of the previous decade. Wrigley Field was not the "Friendly Confines" at that point in our baseball history.

From 1951 through '59, Sox attendance was over a million in all but one season. The Sox were in the ascendancy. We South Siders finally could say in truth, "The Sox are better than the Cubs." And the glory came to a crescendo when the Sox made it to the World Series in 1959, the first time since 1919.

There was more than baseball to make the South Side a joyous place. Times were good. So good that they chased away Depression fears that came down like a shroud during a short-lived recession not long after World War II ended. Some of my friends had been sure that the Depression, which had plagued their lives in the 1930s, would last forever.

But the steel mills were booming. Everything was booming. There was a job for everyone. Some people had two or three jobs. Something bothered me though. The Chicago Motor Coach company took their glamorous, romantic double-deck buses out of service. Forever.

Why did the bus moguls make that unfeeling decision? Because, they said, the double-deckers might have their tops torn off when they rolled under a railroad elevation. Nonsense, we said. The double-deckers had cleared those viaducts for more than 30 years.

Kids, and I was one of them, rode those stately and thrilling buses and none of us was so stupid that we would stand up, up there, and risk having our head knocked off. Our parents would not have liked that.

On those buses I traveled to my "other neighborhood," the Loop. I had become a Loop walker-and-gawker in the early 1940s when I delivered carbon paper and typewriter ribbons for Quest Manufacturing Company.

At a time when I had seen little of the world, I was sure that the real estate we also called "downtown" was the most exciting place in the world. After I had seen a lot of the world, I was still convinced that Chicago's Loop was in a class by itself.

In the early 1950s, I was working in newspaper offices in the Loop. There wasn't much to the Loop then that had not been there before World War II.

Because the longest, deepest Depression in American history had been followed by a long war, the skyline had not changed. The buildings that had been there when I was a kid, still were there. There was no new construction.

There was another reason why Chicago could not keep up with builders in New York City. By ordinance, Chicago architects had to observe a height limit. That rule inhibited those who dreamed of skyscrapers.

Then somebody spoke a magic word to Chicago's first-term mayor, a chubby, jowly fellow named Dick Daley. The word was SETBACKS. The word was magic.

Anyone walking in the Loop in the twenty-first century can see how those setbacks work. And they can see the buildings soar far above 40 stories.

Dick Daley was the "unlikely" mayor. There were

five daily newspapers in Chicago then. Only one endorsed Daley when he made his first run for the office in City Hall. I'm still pleased that the *Chicago-American* was the one that supported Daley. I was writing for the *American* then.

Daley surprised everybody by proving that he knew how to get the job done. He took control of the City Council, whose members had been out of control during the term of his predecessor, Martin Kennelly.

Daley made the Loop cleaner and grander. Dal-

ey made the city better. It was a joy again to saunter through the Loop. Daley was a South Sider. Daley was a lifelong Sox fan. Everything came together in the 1950s.

Bill Gleason was a Chicago sportswriter for 50 years, including stints at the Chicago Sun-Times *and* Southtown Economist.

Above: *Prudential Building, c.1958*
Photograph by Rubin Goldman

Riding the Rails | Raymond DeGroote

I've been going to the Loop since 1937, when I was just seven years old. Riding the "L" was great fun, and as a kid I would always sit in the front of the car so I could watch the view through the window. I can still remember the smell of the candy factories as the train would approach the Loop, right around Franklin Street, just north of the Merchandise Mart. The Holloway Candy Company was there, and you could always smell the chocolate and caramel in the air. That was a good smell, but I also remember the bad smell when I came up from the State Street Subway. If the wind was coming from the southwest it would bring the scent of the stockyards, and that could be very unpleasant.

I began working in the Loop in 1948, and on hot days I would try to ride to work on one of the CTA's "gate" cars. There was a small platform on the back of each gate car, about three feet wide, and you could stand outside and feel the breeze and watch the scenery. It was great fun, and it was an especially nice place to stand if it was hot outside — everybody would crowd onto that back platform and try to muscle their way in! I would also ride the subway to work — it was so much cooler down there — and a good way to beat the heat, too. Of course, in those days there was no air conditioning in the cars, just open windows, but the problem with windows in the subway was all the noise. Riding today may seem noisy, but people should have tried it in those days, particularly as the trains went around the curves!

I still remember the sound of the bell signals that the conductors would ring on the old trains. You see, on a six-car train of gate cars, one conductor had to work in between each of the six cars to manually open and close the gates to allow people on and off. Then, in order for the train to start safely, the motorman had to wait until he heard all the conductor's signal bells indicating it was safe to proceed. All of this has been mechanized today, but not at that time. It worked like this: as soon as the train had finished loading and unloading all of its passengers, the most rear conductor, once he saw that all the gates were secure, would ring his bell twice. Then, the next conductor down the line would ring his bell twice, and so on up the line. Finally, the conductor in the lead car would ring his bell twice, and the train would move. Believe me, service is a lot faster today now that all of this has been mechanized! It was Mayor Daley who ordered all of these old, wooden cars to be replaced by the modern cars, so by the early 1960s most were gone. During the rush hours, however, they would still be pressed into service, and I would always try to ride one of these old cars. The wooden cars tended to creak, and by today's standards it would be quite funny to watch them "rock and roll" down the line.

After World War II, there was an active movement for years to get rid of the elevated tracks around the Loop, and in particular, the tracks above Wabash Avenue. People would say, "It's dirty, gloomy and noisy!" People really thought they could "improve" Wabash and the rest of downtown by tearing down the elevated tracks, and moving them underground. The whole idea seems absurd today because the Loop "L" is the pride of the city. But there was a lot of talk about "modernizing" things in the 1950s, much of it good but some ideas didn't make a lot of sense.

The Loop had a different feel in those days, with newspaper stands and vendors on the street. There were also street photographers taking pictures on the sidewalks, usually of tourists and out-of-towners. I would always try to avoid them! What they would do is take your picture and then hand you an envelope. If you wanted the photo you would send them money — probably a dollar in those days. These guys were around for years, so I guess the pictures couldn't be too bad.

Of course, the 1950s was the era of luxury passenger trains, and all of the major railroads had their ticket offices in the Loop. This is where you would have made your travel plans and bought tickets for your trips. They were very attractive offices with big, scenic posters on the walls featuring the different destinations. After the war, railroad travel was quite popular, and these posters really did beckon one to travel to these places. I rode the Broadway Limited to New York and the Panama Limited to New Orleans, and it is sad the era of these great trains has passed.

Just like today, there were street musicians in the Loop back then, too, but they weren't as loud as they are now! I also remember somebody known as the "Chicken Man" was a presence in the Loop. He had a trained chicken he led around the street on a string, and would perform tricks for money — similar to an organ grinder and a monkey.

Working in the Loop was fun, and I would always try to take advantage of being downtown. Occasionally, I would do my grocery shopping at Hillman's at Randolph and State, which was a very popular place to go. During lunch I would run errands, go shopping or pay my light, gas or electric bills. It was quite natural for people working in the east Loop to go over to Grant Park during their lunch time, particularly for young people. It was a nice place to meet people, or go as a group from my office. I would also go to one of the many cafeterias in the Loop, like the Forum Cafeteria or Harding's — they had the best corned beef and cabbage there! I loved the wiener snitzel at the Berghoff or any German dish at the Old Heidelburg. If we really wanted to splurge, we'd go to Carson Pirie Scott to the restaurant there.

On special occasions you could go to the Prudential Building to the Top of the Rock Restaurant. The view was beautiful, and it was the tallest building in Chicago at the time. I've always thought that the view of the city from the Prudential was better than either the Hancock Building or Sears Tower because of the vantage point. When looking out from the Prudential you could really see the architecture of the other buildings — how they were constructed and all the details close-up. At the Sears Tower you are up so high that when you look down you can hardly see anything — all the details are lost. When the Prudential was constructed it was the first major building to be built after the war. There was much excitement when it was built, and I remember watching the construction from Grant Park as it went up — the same with the Standard Oil Building when it was built.

Everybody always knew each other in the office buildings we worked in, including the elevator starters. All the buildings had starters, whose job it was to supervise the elevator operators as they went up and down. If a building was busy, he could override the controls to bring an elevator down "express" to keep up with the flow. It was like this throughout the Loop. I remember one year there was an elevator strike, and we had to walk 18 floors up to our offices. Fortunately, our business had a ground floor office, too, so the older workers congregated there and tried to conduct business. The rest of us packed our lunches and everything we needed for the day and marched up the stairs.

I think it was more fun working in those days. Now, it seems we all just collect our money and go home. We had pressure on us back then, but not like there is now. People were more helpful and worked together — we had to rely on each other because the

technology wasn't what it is today. A good example of this is long distance phone-calling. In those days, it was very expensive and somewhat difficult to do, so if we were going to call cross-country we'd say, "I'm going to call our office in San Francisco. Does anybody else need to talk to them?" Then, five or six people would line up to call and talk on the same nickel.

Raymond DeGroote is a transportation expert living on the Far North Side. He recently retired from the freight transportation industry.

Above: *Elevated Station in the Loop, c.1955*

The City of Crossroads

Railyards Behind LaSalle Street Station, 1955

Union Station, 1959

LaSalle Street Station, c.1950

Train From Union Station Approaches Canal Street, 1950
Photograph by Bill Sturm *Chicago Sun-Times*

A Few Favorite Restaurants | Eric Bronsky

My interest in restaurants started at an early age, mainly because of the business my father was in — the General Cabinet Company. He made store fixtures and cabinetry for commercial businesses and restaurants, and we went to a lot of these places before, during and after construction. We also went out to dinner at least twice a week, mainly to give my mother a break from cooking every night. Our family was such that just about all of our activities revolved around eating or meal times.

My taste buds have a photographic memory from this period, and my favorite was Don Roth's Blackhawk on Wabash. I started eating there as a kid, downstairs, in what was called the Indian Room. It had a mixture of Art Deco and Indian motifs. I would always order the great roast beef sandwiches or the spaghetti with meat sauce. The Indian Room was closed in the early 1960s and reopened as the Frontier Room. I can still picture it — a lot of wild west-type kitsch — the carpeting had boots and spurs, with a lasso here and there for good measure. There was a spectacular mural on the east wall with a wild west scene, and a stockade made of logs divided the restaurant in the middle. I remember they used to have an Indian chief who would come to your table and pose with your group for a souvenir photograph. I remained a regular costumer into adulthood, when I would eat upstairs, often ordering the prime rib or the famous Spinning Bowl salad. Of course, they would always give the famous speech as they prepared the Spinning Bowl salad, "We toss it only three times, so as not to bruise the tender greens!"

A lot of other great restaurants were also on Wabash, which was situated right between the State Street department stores and fine arts-oriented Michigan Avenue, creating a natural corridor for many very good and some not-so-good restaurants. The Streamliner, on the northeast corner of Lake and Wabash, was known more for the ambiance than the food, because it had a great view of the "L" as it curved around the bend. I became really interested in trains from sitting there as all the trains went by, like the North Shore Line's Electroliners. The name of the restaurant was probably inspired by the cars that went around the building — very 1950s.

There used to be many cafeterias downtown until about the mid-1960s, when they fell out of favor. My favorite was the Ontra Cafeteria, located on the east side of Wabash south of the Blackhawk. You could have an elaborate meal there for a very small price. Probably the most distinctive thing about Loop dining then was that there were many more of these "mom-and-pop" kind of restaurants, because it was before the big chains moved in. There were some chains around the city, though, and a few restaurants that were under the same owner with multiple locations, like Thompson's or Harding's cafeterias, but not too many.

You could say there were two kinds of downtown restaurants in the 1950s — men's and women's. Stouffer's, next to the Trailways bus depot, was a women's restaurant, in that they had many feminine touches, and the food was served in smaller portions, like soufflés and salads. My mother would take me there against my will! I remember ordering the macaroni and cheese there, which you can still buy today in grocery stores. Heather House, on the 8th floor of Carson Pirie Scott, was very popular with women. It was a classy place, with live piano music played there during the lunch hour.

In the 30 North Michigan Building, on the Wabash side, was a place called DeMet's. It was part of a large chain famous for their chocolate candies — especially their turtles. It later became the location of the Marquette Inn.

On the west side of Wabash near Jackson was a great Hungarian restaurant called Epicurean — just enormous portions of food there! I'd get chicken paprikash there with kolacki for dessert. The restaurant was unusual in that it was very narrow and long — only wide enough for two tables abreast.

Another one on Wabash was Paulsen's, which was famous for their soda fountain. They had great sandwiches and ice cream, and there was always a long line during lunch hour in the 1950s. The decor was a cross between Art Deco and Art Moderne, with a huge neon marquee depicting an ice cream sundae that hung over the sidewalk reading, "From a snack to a meal."

Keep in mind that "lunch rooms," later known as "fast food," were more common in the west Loop and on the north and south fringes, mainly because there were more factory and office workers in these locations. Tourists and the well-healed sought the fine dining establishments that were clustered mainly around the theaters, hotel and department store dining rooms in the Loop. A good example is the Italian Village — you could write a book about Italian Village! It hasn't changed at all after all these years. There are three levels, and we would always eat upstairs at the restaurant called The Village. It is very quaint — it looks like a miniature village — some of the booths there look like little houses, complete with roofs above them.

The Berghoff hasn't changed much either. Amazingly, some of the waiters that served me 30 years ago still remember me. I must have tried everything on the menu over the years, but I think the saurbrauten is my favorite. Of course, they had a lot more fried and heavy dishes in those days that are no longer on the menu. On Fridays they had a mostly seafood lunch menu, including an Atlantic Sole filet deep fried in beer batter — who knows how much cholesterol that had! The old-time waiters at the Berghoff were amazingly efficient and agile. They seldom used trays, but balanced multiple entrees and side dishes on one towel-clad arm. They would zoom in and out of the kitchen and somehow manage to plunk the right dishes in front of the right person while barely breaking stride. The Berghoff later opened a second restaurant on Wabash in what was the Ontra Cafeteria. It was very short-lived, as Loop dining went into a state of decline in the 1970s, when dinner business wasn't nearly as brisk as the lunch business.

Henrici's was a huge barn of a place — room after room after room. Even though it closed in 1963 I can still picture the place! They had a big bakery counter in front — they did all their baking on-site. My mother used to go there in the 1940s after seeing a movie and a stage show — this is what everybody did because it was located in the heart of the Randolph Street theater district. A detail I will always remember about the restaurant is that they had supermarket-like automatic doors for the waiters and servers to use as they brought out huge trays of food to the customers. My father was a meat-and-potato type person and would always get the steak or pot roast there. I still have a Henrici's menu from 1958 which shows what a great selection they had to choose from. The menus at many of these bigger restaurants back then were enormous, with hot or cold appetizers, a variety of salads or soups, side dishes, bread baskets, and something called "From the cold buffet" which was a selection of salads, cheeses, fruit and cold meats — you could order a platter of this. Henrici's closed in 1963 to make way for the Daley Center. After the closing date was announced people began stealing

their monogrammed silverware for souvenirs so they actually had to close early because they didn't have enough silverware to operate!

Another really neat place near there was the Mayflower Restaurant on Dearborn, on what today is known as Block 37. In the window they had a donut-making machine where you could watch them frying in the oil and then go down a conveyer belt for cooling and then get coated with frostings and toppings. Always a long line there on Saturdays!

Then there was Fritzels — I have vivid memories of the place — the first things you noticed when you walked in there were the crowds, the piano music, and the perpetual haze from the cigarette smoke! It was boisterous and people went there to see and be seen — lots of movers and shakers. The food was fantastic — they had an onion bread that was second to none. They had things on the menu that you just don't see these days: baked capon, steamed jumbo frankfurters and fantastic chopped liver.

While this was an era that predated the kind of family entertainment restaurants that we see today, one along those lines I do remember is the Kungsholm Swedish Restaurant. This was a Swedish smorgasbord restaurant known more for its famous puppet opera performances than its food. It was considered a landmark type of entertainment for both children and adults — of course these puppets predated the animatronics we see today. The puppets were worked from below the stage using various controls while they used to play famous operas and operettas as a soundtrack. They had extremely elaborate sets — they just boggled the mind! I remember seeing "Hansel and Gretel" and "Goldilocks and the Three Bears" there, but my memories of the food are not as good. It was not kid-friendly food, and a lot of the things looked and tasted strange to me. I remember once when the server came to the table she asked, "How is everything?" I was rather outspoken as a eight-year-old and replied, "I'd like to see a horse eat this!" My parents looked at me in utter shock and the server was speechless!

Eric Bronsky is an architectural modelbuilder who has constructed scale models for the City of Chicago and local architectural firms. He also manufactures models of electric interurban cars that once operated in the city.

Remembering the Movie Palaces | Richard Sklenar

I grew up in the Washington Heights neighborhood. It was a quiet, residential area with mostly single family housing, almost backwater if you will, and there was no local movie theater there. We had to get on a bus at 103rd Street and go east to Michigan Avenue, then go south to Roseland at 111th and State Street. There were three theaters in the area: the State Theater, which was my favorite, the Parkway and the Roseland. Back then, movies were shown in continuous performance. It wasn't like today when you arrive at the theater at a specific time. Instead, you went to the theater whenever you wanted to and stayed until the movie got back to the point you began watching.

As a kid, we only went to the downtown theaters on special occasions. The first time I was ever in the Chicago Theater was during the holidays. I was with a friend and his mother, and while she shopped at Marshall Field's, we saw a movie. It was crowded, and the ushers directed us upstairs to the balcony. Well, we went up and up and up and up and finally, somewhere near the top, we found seats. When I turned around and looked back at where I had traveled from it was just mind-boggling — the theater was so huge! Way down somewhere was the movie screen — and they had one of the biggest screens in the city! The theater made a big impression on me, and I remember the Chicago Theater above any other theater I have been in.

The United Artists Theater on Randolph Street, which was a part of theater row, was wonderfully lit by neon and light bulbs — from 9:00 in the morning to closing — with lights blazing all day long. Back then, Balaban and Katz had their own sign department, and they would create these large, painted false fronts. Pictures would always open in the Loop first, and would stay there for four to six weeks exclusively before they opened in the neighborhoods. So, they created these elaborate, oversized displays to advertise the movies and their stars. I remember walking by the theater and being impressed by the display that stretched the whole length of the building — almost 75 feet long.

The Oriental Theater is a wonderfully ornamented theater, but back in the 1950s it was very dark and not maintained very well. After it was renovated a few years ago, I saw details that I didn't remember from the past. But back then going to the movies was common place, and we didn't notice the details. We were going to the movies on such a regular basis, particularly before television, that one theater was just like the next. The movies changed in the neighborhoods once a week, and sometimes two or three times a week. So, we didn't look at the walls after a while.

My first experience with Cinerama was on a Cub Scout trip to the Palace Theater, next to the Bismarck Hotel. Cinerama was a special wide screen process that was filmed with three cameras and played back with three separate projectors. So, it required a huge, curved screen to be installed before movies could be shown. The screens were so large, on a 120 degree radius, that they covered up a lot of a theater's plaster work and the organ chamber. I sat in the third row of the balcony that day, and the movie we saw was "This is Cinerama," narrated by Lowell Thomas. The opening scene was of a roller coaster going up a hill and then, all of sudden, it went sweeping down — I felt like I was going to fall out of my seat! It was spectacular! Widescreen movies were a direct reaction to television, which had caused a decline in revenues at the box office. They were going to show us things on a giant screen that you could never see on a tiny television screen.

The Loop Theater on State Street was very successful in the 1960s, but it was originally known as the Telenews Theater. Many people might remember the famous cigarette company sign that had huge puffs of smoke right next to it. The Telenews had about 650 seats and a small balcony, and was one of two newsreel theaters in the city, the other called The Today. They both ran newsreels constantly, about a one-hour program. Before television, if you wanted to see images from the major news stories of the day, you went to these theaters. All the major movie studios had divisions that made newsreel footage, and they sent photographers all over the world. Within hours they could have that footage developed and on the screen — maybe not in Chicago but certainly in New York. It's hard to imagine such a thing today with CNN and other instant news sources.

Something else to remember — most people today have not been in a movie palace to see it operating as a movie palace. Very few people have ever sat in a theater with 3000 people to see a movie, and that is a totally different experience. There is a whole lot of energy created when you are laughing together with that many people, or if it's sad, crying with that many people. I wonder what the psychology of all of this might be — so many people sharing a common experience at a theater, compared to watching a television program alone. There was a sense of community to these experiences then, and I'm afraid that might be lost today.

Richard Sklenar is executive director of the Theater Historical Society of America.

"This is Cinerama," Palace Theater, 1956

A Day to Remember

Photographed by a tourist, these snapshots of Loop theaters were all made on a single summer day in 1953. The Oriental Theater is the only one remaining.

A Christmas Tradtion | Mary Robinson Kalista

My mother, Lucile Ward Robinson, a WPA muralist and artist, began creating displays at Marshall Field's in the early 1950s. It was a big part of my life in those years. I would go downtown, even when I was only nine or ten years old, and help her in the display department on the twelfth and thirteenth floors. I was allowed to paste gold trim on the Christmas ornaments, choose lace for parasols, and put ribbons and other decorations on the large rabbits created for her Easter display in the main aisle of the toy department, also known as Candy Cane Lane during the Christmas season.

Planning was exciting, and in our family we often sat around the dinner table, dreaming about and discussing the next project. Once decided upon, my mother would draw up the designs in scale, choosing paint colors, fabrics, etc. The drawings were then given to the display department carpenters, painters and upholsterers, many of whom were Old World craftsmen who had apprenticed in Germany. They would follow her plans, building whatever was needed. It was all "one of a kind." Nowadays, Field's and other large department stores simply go to display companies who provide ready-made displays with mechanized characters included.

Preparations for all of the well-known Christmas displays — the Christmas tree in the Walnut Room, the State Street windows, Candy Cane Lane in the Children's Department on the fourth floor, the Narcissus fountain in the Narcissus Dining Room on the seventh floor — began in May or June. The themes and designs for all of these were completely different each year. Previous displays were never reused.

One of my mother's most exciting projects was Cozy Cloud Cottage, the Christmastime residence of Santa Claus, on the seventh floor. (During the rest of the year, this house of four or more rooms was known as the Trend House and it displayed fine furniture.) On the Saturday after Thanksgiving, Santa would arrive in Chicago at the end of the Christmas parade. He would proceed to Cozy Cloud Cottage and, assisted by Aunt Holly and Uncle Mistletoe, he would discuss the wish lists of hundreds of children, who would sit on his lap and be photographed with him for posterity. Many may remember that waiting to see Santa in the long, colorfully painted, wooden maze seemed interminable.

The year that my mother designed Cozy Cloud Cottage was very exciting for my brother and me, and even our friends, whose names were also included in the large "Book of Good Girls and Boys" placed next to Santa's big chair. That year, as you waited in the maze, you saw a landing strip with the Aurora Borealis in the background. Homing pigeons were arriving with letters from children all over the world. The first room was Santa's mailroom where the letters were being sorted and read. As you arrived in the second room, there was a huge cross section of an igloo with the North Pole in the center. This was Santa's workshop and a mechanized Santa would periodically go to the top of the pole with his spyglass and move in a circular motion to look for good boys and girls. On the right side of the igloo there were three floors where angels were baking and making dolls and other Christmas delights for little girls and on the left side there were gnomes making horseshoes for Santa's reindeer and toys for little boys. At the bottom of Santa's pole two gnomes were turning a winch to mechanically raise him to the top. Mechanized displays like this were produced by display companies like Sylvestri, who created these figures from the artist's own designs. After touring the house and seeing Santa, one exited through the Penguin Snack Bar, where there were penguins on little bar stools. On the bar there were amusing signs that my father came up with, like "Don't Honk for Service" and "Formal Attire Required," and the menu consisted of exotic North Pole cocktails and snacks.

Marshall Field's, of course, was more than just holidays — it was really "downtown" for many. The third floor Waiting Room was a fixture — anyone who wanted to meet someone downtown would designate the third floor Waiting Room." It was a comfortable place, right by the escalators, with large leather chairs and elegant marble-clad washrooms. People could rest there, visit there, read there, or just people watch. Certainly the Waiting Room was a better place to meet than outside under the clock, when the weather was questionable.

The fourth floor was legendary, a paradise for children. I remember it as if I had lived there. They had a selection of Madame Alexander dolls, doll trunks filled with outfits, doll houses with every kind of furniture imaginable, clothes washers that really worked, and more. For boys, there were lead soldiers, train sets, Lincoln Logs and elaborate Erector sets, and for everyone, a log cabin playhouse. The entire fourth floor was for kids! There was also a camp sec-

Marshall Field's Candy Cane Lane, 1953
Marshall Field's Archive

tion where you could buy everything you needed for summer camp, including the name tags to sew into your outfits. My mother did a beautiful mural for that department, a scene of the woods with animals, birds and wild flowers, and it remained for many years because the head of the camp section would never let it be painted out

I remember so much — lunch in the Walnut Room, choosing stamps and coins on the third floor, and the fabulous book department. The first floor was elegance personified — floor walkers in dark suits and ties, precious jewels, fine china and silver, perfume, and the latest accessories — Field's had it all!

Mary Robinson Kalista, educator, is the granddaughter of J. C. Robinson, the architect of the Chicago Cultural Center.

The Loop's Jazz and Nightclubs | Joe Levinson

During the 1950s, there was a wide variety of nightclubs and music venues in downtown Chicago and the Near North Side. Of course, the Loop movie palaces still offered great entertainment, including the Oriental Theater on Randolph Street. It was a terrific showcase for vaudeville acts on stage between the motion pictures that were featured there. Many great comedians, dog acts, plate twirlers, song-and-dance teams and other remnants of earlier vaudeville from the '20s worked the Oriental. The Chicago Theater on State Street was another important venue for entertainment. The biggest names in show business appeared there, as well as the first-run films from Hollywood. I remember when Dean Martin and Jerry Lewis were there — they nearly caused a riot because of the huge crowds of fans trying to get in or get their autographs. I saw Jack Benny there, as well as George Burns and Gracie Allen. It was a magical place.

Another theater, of a very different nature, was the Rialto Theater on State Street at Van Buren. For years it was a burlesque venue, and then during the war it changed its name to The Downtown, where they featured many of the nation's greatest black dance bands on stage, including vaudeville acts. I saw Cab Calloway's band with Dizzy Gillespie in the trumpet section there. I also saw Andy Kirk and His 12 Clouds of Joy. Later, I saw the absolute greatest black dance band that ever played: Jimmy Lunceford's Orchestra.

For jazz, the Blue Note on Randolph was extremely popular. The biggest names worked there, including Duke Ellington, Dizzie Gillespie, Harry James, Charley Barnet, The Sauter-Finnigan Band, Dave Brubeck, and Les Brown. There was just an amazing array of artists who appeared there, and it became known as one of the world's greatest jazz rooms. The Brass Rail, also located on Randolph, featured small jazz groups like Count Basie's sextet and the Dukes of Dixieland. Also nearby was the Prevue Lounge, a showcase for traveling jazz artists like Al Cohn and Zoot Sims.

One of the most popular downtown clubs was the London House, located on the southwest corner of Michigan and Wacker, in the London Guarantee Building. The place served top-flight steaks and chops and had the world's greatest jazz players performing there. I saw Oscar Peterson's trio with Ray Brown on bass, George Shearing's quintet with Marjie Hyams on vibes, Woody Herman's septet, Andre Previn's trio and, believe it or not, Spike Jones and the City Slickers played there. You name it — the best small bands in the world

were booked at the London House. I actually played at the London House on what were known as "off-nights," Sundays and Mondays, either when the featured acts were not working, or sometimes to alternate with them on stage. Performers on off-nights included Audrey Morris and Judy Roberts, and the Ramsey Lewis Trio was the house band for many years. Another long-running, off-night pianist was Eddie Higgins, regarded today as one of the world's premiere jazz artists.

Of course, many of the city's downtown hotels had nightclubs and ballrooms in the '50s, including the Knickerbocker Hotel on Walton Street, right across from the Drake Hotel. On the hotel's first floor was a large ballroom that featured a glass dance floor with built-in colored lighting. For years, this room was a public nightclub as well as a place for high school proms. The glass floor still exists today, and the room is now used for private parties.

One of the most famous places was the Panther Room in the Sherman Hotel, on the site of what became the Thompson Center on Randolph Street. This hotel was a mainstay for out-of-towners and "hot pillow" trysts of the businessmen's crowd. The Panther Room, with its dinner and showroom, regularly featured big name bands for both listening and dancing. I "saw" Woody Herman's First Herd at the Panther Room in 1945. I was too young at that time to enter the room by myself, and since I only had a few cents in my pocket I couldn't have afforded anything. So, instead, I stood in the doorway and listened to the music, and admired my musical heroes who included Chubby Jackson, Don Lamond, Conte Condoli, Flip Phillips and the rest of that exciting band. The maitre'd would spot me and tell me to get lost, but I would just wait a while and come right back to the door. On another night, I saw Jimmy Dorsey's band play at the Panther Room and I was enamored with his popular girl vocalist, Helen O'Connell, who, along with Bob Eberly, charmed the dancers with the popular songs of the day. I actually heard her sing her big hit "Green Eyes" while standing in the doorway of the Panther Room.

There were also many clubs north of the Loop, on the Near North Side, like the Gaslight Club, which opened in 1952. It featured "hot" dixieland bands, and became a gathering spot for young people who were seeking a sophisticated good time. The club had a line of women who dressed like frontier dance hall girls in the Old West, and the dixieland band dressed like barrel house band players and accompanied them in their routines. The club was housed in a multi-story house that had numerous rooms for small groups of guests, with paintings of scantily-clad women on the walls.

Down the street was Mister Kelly's on Rush at Elm. It was a wildly popular place to eat great chops and see and hear the greatest singers and comedians perform. Ella Fitzgerald, Sarah Vaugh, Victor Borge, Mort Sahl, Lenny Bruce, Shelley Berman and dozens of other name acts worked the room during its years of operation. Standing room was the name of the game on weekends just to get in at Mister Kelly's. I played for several of the acts that worked there but never for Ella or Sarah — they came with their own well-rehearsed trios. On many occasions I found a little corner at the back of the room and stood there listening to and admiring Ella and Sarah's expertise — and learning! Many years later, in the 1970s, I played at Mister Kelly's in a trio backing Bette Midler. It was one of the funniest experiences of my life, and I wound up with stomach aches from laughing as she did her act.

When Kaye Ballard, the singer-comedienne from New York, was featured at Mister Kelly's, I was in the backup trio with Marty Rubenstein and Jack Noren. We rehearsed her during the afternoon, but I was totally unprepared for her opening night entrance. We started a vamp and Marty got on his microphone and said, "And now, direct from the phone booth on the corner, here's Kaye Ballard!" Well, she trounced through the crowded tables to great applause, climbed onto the little stage and showed off an enormously long purple boa, wrapped around her shoulders. So, we kept up the vamp we were playing, waiting for her to start singing her first number. Well, she stood there grinning toothfully at the crowd who were gasping at the ridiculous boa that she wore. Finally, she said, "You like it? S&H Green Stamps bought it!" Then she threw it behind her and Marty and Jack started playing her opener. But I couldn't play because the boa flew back and wound itself right around the neck of my bass, blocking my fingers from playing anything! The audience was roaring with laughter and so were Marty and Jack. Finally, she turned around and saw what was happening — I was frantically trying to unwind the boa. "Stop the music," she shouted, "Let's keep it in the act!" So, every night for her three-week run, she tried to replicate that opening night boa toss, but each time it landed on the drums, the piano, out in the audience, everywhere but around the neck of my bass. She was absolutely a dynamite performer and we all loved her.

The Happy Medium, a two-story showcase for entertainment, was located on Rush Street across from Mister Kelly's. In the basement they had a music bar, and on the street-level there was a tiny theater with a raised proscenium stage, opposite about ten rows of seats. Little theater productions were featured there as well as singers and dancers. In 1963, I played bass in the quartet that backed the production of "Jacques Brel Is Alive and Well and Living in Paris." The show was an instant success, and after it finally ended its run, two years later, I realized that I'd played 488 performances. I had to alternate every other week with another bass player to save my sanity!

Another Rush Street venue was the Gate of Horn, which became one of the country's most famous folk music showcases. I remember seeing the Kingston Trio there as well as Odetta. Also on Rush Street was the Hotel Maryland, which had the Cloister Inn Lounge in the lower level of the hotel. This dimly-lit lounge featured a piano bar where Dick Marx and Johnny Frigo played with Lurlean Hunter, one of Chicago's greatest jazz vocalists.

Of course, the Pump Room at the Ambassador East Hotel was a very popular venue during the war years and after. The John Kirby Sextet played in the back of the room where they had a dance floor and bandstand. One of the local radio stations broadcast the Kirby Sextet live from there at night, and they were one of the finest little jazz groups that ever happened — their arrangements were spectacular! Charlie Shavers, trumpet player and arranger, used to take classical music pieces and "swing" them. The dance floor would be filled with people in those years — they loved to dance to that little band!

Across the street, at the Ambassador West Hotel, they had a small room located off the lobby called the Buttery. It was a very intimate bar that featured a magician who did tabletop magic tricks for the guests. There was also a little four-piece band in there that was led by a pianist with the amazing name of Romeo Meltz. They played mostly Latin music, and a lot of people came to the Buttery to hear them. The club was also very popular with salesmen because of the call girls who frequented the club. Of course, you wouldn't know what was going on unless you were there every night — or you worked in the band!

Joe Levinson has pursued a lifelong love of jazz music and continues to play his bass fiddle around the city.

Booth One

Ernie Byfield opened the Pump Room in the Ambassador East Hotel in 1938. By the 1950s, it was a magnet for national celebrities and socialites, with Booth One becoming one of the most reknowned dining tables in the country.   Private Collection

Left: *Alfred Hitchcock*

Above: *Bob Hope and Jane Russell*

Left: *Janet Leigh and Tony Curtis*

Above: *Robert Wagner and Natalie Wood*

Left: *Kim Novak*

Above: *Mickey Rooney*

Right: *Ernie Banks*

'Just a Special Place' | Bob Dauber

I went downtown quite a bit when I was growing up, and I took the "L" to get there, starting when I was only nine years old. My primary purpose for going downtown was to take piano lessons at the Chicago Conservatory of Music, located next door to Roosevelt University in the Fine Arts Building. After my lessons I would walk down Wabash Avenue and look at all the signs and stores and wonder what went on in those places — it was pretty overwhelming for a kid!

My mother used to drag me downtown to go shopping at Marshall Field's, and she used to love to take me to the restaurants there. I remember the Walnut Room and the Narcissus Room, and one of them served this absolutely world-class corned beef hash — that was a major, major treat to eat. While my mother was shopping, I would go to the sporting goods department and play. We gravitated there because, as kids, we didn't want to stand around the women's lingerie department.

My first job in the Loop was at Mandel Brothers in the men's furnishings department. We sold men's shirts and ties, and there were more expensive furnishings in glass cases. I made $1.10 an hour and 1% commission on the job. I remember the time two men came into the store and one of them wanted to look at some ties in the glass case. Even at the 1% commission, you hustled as much as you could because it was a few more cents in your pocket if you made the sale. One of the men was very well dressed in a camel hair coat and a nice fedora, and the other guy was sort of chubby. The nicely dressed guy went through every tie in the glass case, and I used up a great deal of time with him. After what seemed like 20 minutes, I said to him, "Sir, if you don't see anything that you like here, why don't you go down the street to Sears!" He gave me a really scary look, and then he and the other guy left the store. There was a young lady I worked with in the department, and she came over and said, "If I were you, I'd go hide in the stockroom for the rest of the day. Do you know who you just told to go to Sears? That was a member of the Mob!" I said, "I'll see you in the stockroom!"

In the 1950s, it was still a special thing to go downtown, especially on a date, since it was much more expensive. The Loop was just a special place for us to go — it was out of the neighborhood — an adventure — and it was upscale. It was less expensive to take a date to neighborhood theater or club, but on special occasions we went to the downtown clubs, like Mister Kelly's, the Black Orchid, London House and the Blue Note.

I remember the time we went to the Blue Note after my senior prom to hear Duke Ellington. On our way there, I said to my girlfriend, "It's going to be great to see the Duke again." She said, "Do you know him?" I said, "Sure!" So, we went to the Blue Note, and who was standing at the maitre d' stand but Duke Ellington. He took a look at me and said, "Man, how are you doing, great to see you." My girlfriend looked like her jaw was going to hit the floor. I said, "It's good to see you." I couldn't have scripted it any better, especially when you consider the fact that he didn't even know me. It was just one of those very happy accidents.

I always loved going to the Chicago Theater. When I started going there, it cost about $.75, while it cost only $.25 at the Granada Theater on Sheridan and Devon in Rogers Park. But for $.75, you could see a great movie and a top notch stage show. You'd see some of the greatest stars of the day, like Martin and Lewis, Bob Hope, Danny Thomas, Spike Jones, Cab Calloway, and an endless procession of jugglers and gymnasts — like the folks who used to appear on the "Ed Sullivan Show" on Sunday nights. The stage show usually followed a single movie feature at the Chicago, and quite often the stars who were in the movie also appeared on stage. I was at one of the last stage shows at the Chicago in the late 1950s and one of the performers was Edie Gorme. Her husband, Steve Lawrence, was in the Service, and, on another occasion when she was performing at the Chez Paree, he made a surprise appearance at Edie's show still wearing his military uniform.

Other places you could see a great show included the Black Orchid, located off Michigan Avenue around Superior. I remember going there to see Johnny Mathis in 1958 — he was a big star by then. His warm-up act was a guy I'd never heard of before, Professor Irwin Corey, billed as "The World's Foremost Authority." He came out wearing a beat-up tuxedo and was rather disheveled looking. He would walk back and forth across the stage and wouldn't say a word, but appeared to be deep in thought. Eventually, he looked like he was about to say something, but then he would start walking back and forth all over again. This continued until, finally, he shouted his famous opening line — "However..." That was always the opening line to his act.

Bob Dauber is a creative consultant who helped develop the popular children's character "Barney" for television.

Crowds Gather for the First Showing of "Little Egypt," 1951

3 GROWING UP IN THE CITY

During the 1950s, Chicago was a great place to grow up. The neighborhoods were vibrant and vital places, and children were always outside talking, playing or just hanging out. It was an innocent time, and parents didn't worry about supervising their kids constantly; safety was almost never a concern. Kids moved freely throughout their neighborhoods and beyond — to a friend's house, to the corner store, to Riverview Park or even downtown.

As a result of this freedom, kids learned to be independent and resourceful — they had to. Many families were large, and had little money to provide entertainment or fun, so kids had to create their own forms of amusement. They organized their own games, made their own rules, and usually without any budget. Amazingly, despite this lack of funds, nobody ever felt "poor."

By the end of the decade, the lives of this generation would gradually become more complicated, but it was an amazing transition to witness: the birth of television, the rise of rock and roll and the beginning of a sexual revolution. Social change was coming to Chicago, too, as the city began to face the issues of racial inequality and social injustice. For some kids it could be a difficult time, but most were protected from the pain of these issues, if only temporarily, because they would have to be faced in adulthood.

An Age of Innocence

Children growing up in the 1950s didn't have much to worry about. Their neighborhoods were safe, schools were good, and they could travel almost anywhere, including downtown, without concern for safety. But most kids stayed close to home, playing in the yards, streets and playgrounds of their own area. The games that kids played in the '50s remained similar to those that were played in the 1930s and '40s, including marbles, pinners, Rolevio, tag and line ball. In the summer, kids left in the morning with only a "be home for dinner" from their mothers. After they ate, kids returned to their games, playing until dark but usually within ear shot of their parents. To beat the heat, kids played board games on their porches or cooled off at the beach or pool at a local park. During the winter months, kids were still playing outside, including sledding, having snowball fights, or ice skating at the local rinks or flooded backyards of their neighborhood.

Kids saved what little money they could to buy the toys and games they valued most: boys loved comic books, baseball cards and BB guns while girls bought paper dolls, clothes and movie magazines. All children loved to go the local drug stores and sweet shops to buy their favorite treats, like chocolate bars, candy cigarettes and little wax bottles filled with colored syrup. Neighborhood stores had plenty of more expensive toys for kids to dream about as well, whether it be at a dime store or fancy hobby shop. Kids did all sorts of things to raise money for the objects they longed for, including paper routes, collecting bottles for refunds and doing chores for their parents and neighbors.

It was hard for most kids to be bored during the 1950s. The neighborhoods were always abuzz with activity, especially at the local parks and field houses. The Chicago Park District offered an amazing variety of activities for kids, including classes in crafts, music and gardening; competitions in sand craft, marbles, and kite making; and plenty of sports, including baseball, football, basketball and swimming. Many kids "lived" at their local parks, participating in every activity they could, but also enjoying the relative quiet and open space that the parks provided, a necessity for apartment dwellers.

At the park district's Lincoln Park Zoo, kids could see the the animals, ride a miniature train or beginning in 1952, go to the new Children's Zoo. Many city kids were inspired to visit the zoo by watching the local WBKB television program "Zoo Parade," with host Marlin Perkins. The show was eventually picked up by NBC stations around the country, making Perkins a national media figure. "Zoo Parade," and Perkins' later show "Wild Kingdom," helped educate a generation of children about animal life and natural history, and made the Lincoln Park Zoo one of the city's biggest attractions.

While going to the zoo was fun, nothing could compare to the thrills at Riverview Amusement Park. Since 1904, kids had been drawn to the 70 acres of rides and sideshows there, including the Pair-O-Chutes, the Bobs and the Shoot the Chutes. During the summer, kids would scrape together as much money as they could and ride the streetcar to Western and Belmont, where for a relatively small amount of money, they could spend the entire day eating popcorn and having fun — especially if it was a Two-Cent Day.

The domination of Riverview would be challenged by a series of new amusement parks that opened in the area, including Hollywood Kiddieland and Kiddy Town Park in Chicago, Kiddieland Park in Maywood, Fairyland Park in Lyons and Santa's Village in East Dundee. Still, nothing could compare with the history or scale of Riverview, which drew many adults who were brought to the park as children themselves.

Kids loved outdoor activities, but by the late 1940s watching television began to compete for their attention. In the morning, there was "Ding Dong School" with Miss Frances, "Captain Kangaroo" with Bob Keeshan and a host of cartoon shows. While these programs were popular, the high point of the day for children's television was during lunchtime. Most kids hurried home from school to watch "Lunchtime Little Theater" on WGN-TV with Uncle Bucky and Ned Locke or "Noontime Comics" on WNBQ-TV with Uncle Johnny Coons. Beginning in 1961, however, a show that would surpass the popularity of any local children's programming would begin: "Bozo's Circus." The success of lunchtime programing was a phenomenon unique to Chicago, where kids lived in neighborhoods with schools within quick walking distance. In most other cities kids stayed at school for lunch, or didn't have major children's programming air at that time of day. After the school day was over, kids could come home and watch "Garfield Goose," "The Three Stooges," "Howdy Doody" and the popular "Mickey Mouse Club."

Adolescence

As kids grew older, interest turned to the opposite sex, and as early as grammar school kids began participating in kissing parties and went on group dates to movies or ice cream parlors. But these were simple times, so the dating that took place was usually innocent and polite — and seldom very serious. After school each day, kids hung-out together in neighborhood restaurants and pizza parlors, talking, flirting or listening to jukebox music. By high school age, more mature dating began, but the ultimate "black mark" for a girl was being known as "fast" or "easy," so most girls would never let a relationship advance to that level. Nothing could stop boys from making-up stories about their prowess, however, seeming to always "score" or get to "first base." It was only years later that males would admit that their sex lives in the 1950s were much less eventful than they had led their friends to believe.

While the boys talked a good game, most girls just wanted to have fun and socialize, and often dated more than one boy at a time. Couples went to movies, parties or attended a Catholic Youth Organization (CYO), B'nai Brith Youth Organization (BBYO) or school-sponsored parties or dances, with girls usually wearing their best poodle skirt or sweater set. If a boy was lucky enough to have a driver's license and access to a car, he could take a date to one of the new drive-in theaters or restaurants built in the city or suburbs. Car ownership was pretty rare for kids, however, though some boys pooled their money together to buy a "junker" they could fix-up for use on dates.

With the introduction of rock and roll music in the mid-1950s, a whole new world of activities based on music and dancing began for teenagers. Instead of listening to the soft ballads of Patti Page or Frankie Laine, kids started listening to the high-energy songs of Bill Haley and Elvis Presley. The music also led to new radio station formats in Chicago based on rock and roll music, with their own youth-oriented deejays like Howard Miller and Milo Hamilton on WIND-AM. Soon, other stations began gearing their programming to young people, and disc jockeys like Dick Biondi and Clark Weber dominated the airwaves. Jazz and rhythm and blues stations were also becoming popular, as well as their radio personalities, like "Daddy-O" Daylie, Yvonne Daniels and "Symphony" Sid McCoy.

As rock and roll music became more popular kids began to listen and dance to it wherever they could, from their bedrooms to large show halls. CYO and religious organizations held dances in church halls and basements, usually playing records over static-laden loudspeakers for kids to listen and dance to. Public schools and park districts held similar dances in gymnasiums, field houses and auditoriums, often elaborately decorated with streamers and posters. Eventually, as rock and roll music became more popular, radio station or record company sponsored sock hops and concerts began to draw big crowds to concert halls and ballrooms, aided greatly by heavy promotion on radio stations like WCFL, WLS, WJJD and WIND.

Dancing was a favorite activity, and kids, particularly girls, practiced constantly for big weekend events. Teenagers rehearsed the Stroll, Limbo, Cha-Cha, Mashed Potato, Twist and other popular dances trying to perfect their moves — as well as improvise their own steps. When left alone, kids were known to take the slow dances to another level of intimacy, but it was the role of the chaperones, particularly the priests and nuns at the CYO venues, to make sure that no "dirty dancing" took place.

During the 1950s and early '60s many of the pioneers of rock and roll and rhythm and blues held concerts in front of enthusiastic Chicago crowds, including Elvis Presley at the Stadium and Little Richard at the International Amphitheater. Many young men were inspired by these performances to create their own groups — both by the music and the swooning girl's reactions. Following many of these concerts, kids exchanged the accordions and other instruments their parents hoped they would learn for the staples of pop music: electric guitars and basses. Some of these musicians would even go on to national fame, like Jim Peterik of the Ides of March and Ray Manzerek of the Doors.

Coming of Age

For many young men, becoming a man meant seeking a "coming of age" experience, usually in one of the area's red-light districts. On the city's southern border, Calumet City had a reputation for prostitution and other vices, and many kids went there looking for an inexpensive first encounter — and usually finding it. It was a sight to see in those years, with the main entertainment drag featuring loud, racy displays advertising strippers and sex shows. Similar offerings could be found on Chicago's West Side along the 3000 block of Madison Street, where clubs like the Domes, L & L and the Flamingo offered racy shows that went much further than the more reserved downtown clubs.

More then any other experience, however, graduation from high school marked the ascension into adulthood. And the choices most teenagers had as they went out into the world were very different from today. College was not an option for everybody, and for many men careers began at age 18 either in the work force or the military.

For women, the concept of a career beyond raising a family was only beginning. While there were employment opportunities available, most were in fields with limited room for advancement — and career paths on the same level as men were practically nonexistent. Nursing, teaching and secretarial work were all considered traditional paths, and most women were discouraged from jobs or educational pursuits thought "better suited" for men. This would change in the 1960s, like so much else.

Page 110: *North Side High School Students, c.1950*

'Nearly 2000 Mammals, Birds and Reptiles!'

Above: *Chief Whistling Thunder Scouts in Jackson Park, c.1950*
Top Right: *Zoo Director Marlin Perkins in Lincoln Park, c. 1950*
Bottom Right: *Children's Zoo in Lincoln Park, 1957*
Chicago Park District Special Collections

Chicago's Marble Champs

Top Left: *Junior Marble Champ Alex Brown, 1952*

Bottom Left and Above: *Douglas Park Marble Competition, 1951*

Chicago Park District Special Collections

Postcards From Riverview

The Riverview Amusement Park photo studio dates back to the early 1900s, when visitors could have their pictures taken sitting on a smiling half moon. Over the years, the backdrops changed, including a facsimile railroad car, touring car and these bar scenes.

DINTY MOORES

A 'Tom Sawyer' Life in Chatham | Norman Mark

I was born in 1939 and grew up on the West Side until kindergarten, when we moved to the South Side's Chatham neighborhood. In Chatham I lived sort of a "Tom Sawyer" type of existence. I lived at 84th and St. Lawrence, and between 84th and 87th there was a big open field or "prairie." We called it "the swamp" because it was always filled with water, and, all summer long, boys would be coming home with frogs and snakes. Believe it or not, there were people who were putting logs together and charging money to ferry people across the swamp and back! We would play guns there, and get into fights, and when we came home our mothers would make us take off all our clothes outside because we stunk so much.

I went to Dixon Elementary School, and benefited from what I think were the last of the tough, Irish, old maid school teachers: Monaghan, Mahoney, and McDade. They were tough, but they were also good teachers and gave us a good education. Dixon was located at 83rd and Cottage, and I remember that there was a long-standing tradition there: when school was finally let out in June, everybody would take their paint sets and throw them against the same large brick wall — year after year. The resulting mess was actually an amazing piece of modern art!

I remember that in about 6th grade all the boys got together and decided that we would have girlfriends. But we never bothered to tell the girls that we were going to have girlfriends, or that they were our girlfriends, nor did we ever speak to them at all! My girlfriend, and I don't think that I've told her to this day, was Patti Heinemann, of the Heinemann Bakeries, who was a great girlfriend to have.

I didn't get to the Loop very much, so it was a big deal when I did. You had to put on a shirt and tie and itchy, woolen pants — back then you dressed up to go downtown. My dad was a food buyer at Goldblatt's, so for the Christmas parade we would go up to the ninth or tenth floor of the store and stand by the big windows looking down on the parade and inflated balloons. My mother was afraid to drive on the Outer Drive, so she would take State Street all the way downtown. That meant we would stop every three blocks and my brother and I would get nauseous while sitting in the back seat. It seemed like it took hours to get downtown!

I went to Hirsch High School, which was very small, with only about 1200 kids. I remember we had a physics instructor there who was terrible and, finally, in frustration, he walked out on the class. So, we were left in the physics lab by ourselves. There were these big, convex mirrors in the classroom and we shined them down, three floors below, at automobiles to try and blind the drivers!

I also remember a teacher I had in my junior year who was one of the most fearsome English teachers I have ever had in my life — Olga Lawrenz. I was supposed to do an essay on a Mark Twain story, and she made me rewrite it a dozen times. There is no other teacher, living or dead, who would go through reading something that I wrote that many times until I got it right. But she taught me the value of the rewrite.

As for dating, I was very shy, which meant that I walked the same girl home from high school for three years before I asked her out. Finally, I went to the prom with her. There were mixers in high school, and I remember that my mother insisted I get a checkered green cashmere sports jacket. When I would dance with a girl and she realized that the jacket was cashmere, I would get my back scratched. So, that was like a "chick magnet." I remember at Dixon they started after school activities that included dancing classes. We would have hour-long dancing classes in the gymnasium, including the box step, the rhumba, the two-step, and others. I remember one time it was a boy's choice for the dance. So, all the boys went rushing over to the one girl who had developed early "physical" gifts. About that same time it was a fad for certain girls to wear Mickey Mouse tee shirts. Mickey's nose on the tee shirt was a little bulb, and when you squeezed the nose it made a little squeaky sound. So, some of the boys believed that was the natural sound when you touched a girl's chest.

One of my first crushes in childhood was Mary Hartline — she was on "Super Circus" on Sunday afternoons. I lusted after her. In my mind I had a plan, and this is what I was going to do: I had a dog, a mixed breed named Muddy, and the dog was very smart. I created a routine where the dog would lie down, roll over, beg, and jump up and down — all just with hand signals. I was training the dog so that I would get on Mary Hartline's television program, just so she would give me a kiss on the cheek. That was my big, big desire.

Norman Mark is an award-winning journalist, radio and TV broadcaster, and movie reviewer living in California.

Prairie near 85th Street, 1955

Falling Asleep to the Sound of the TV | Bruce DuMont

I was born in New London, Connecticut, in 1944 and came here with my parents in 1949. Initially, I grew up at 831 N. LaSalle Street, right across from the Moody Bible Institute, but then we moved to 3935 W. Diversey, because my mother worked for the Olsen Rug Company. I was out in the far reaches of Logan Square, which, compared with the neighborhood that we had come from, was really nice — there were trees, and I lived right across the street from Kosciusko Park. Of course, only a block away from us was Olsen Falls, run by the Olsen Rug Company. It's kind of hard to imagine today, but the company probably spent hundreds of thousands of dollars to create this beautiful rock garden and falls. It was a wonderful area, and people would come to see it from all over the Midwest. I liked it very much as a young boy, but I think that it was a much bigger deal for people who came there from a great distance. It was just a block away from us, and I remember going there on warm summer nights to enjoy the breeze and the mist from the falls, especially since we didn't have air conditioning. Later on, we got a fan, but I recall it was the blowing mist from Olsen Falls that helped us to keep cool on many hot summer nights.

My interest in television goes back to my tenth birthday, when I went on a father-son trip to New York to see my uncle, Allen DuMont. My uncle was head of the DuMont Television Network at that time, and while visiting him I sat in Captain Video's spaceship — at that point I fell in love with television and have never really wanted to do anything but that since then. It was also during the trip that I realized the studio sets were made of cardboard, and were very inexpensive to make. So, I began to play television — I would take a box, cut out the front and make it into a television set. Sometimes, I would go through the alley behind our apartment on Diversey and get huge boxes to make furniture, sets and carve microphones. There was one summer, when in absolute disciplined form, I would do a half-hour talk show right after the "Bob Crosby Show" and right before "Queen For A Day." I would routinely do an entire 30-minute show, and I would interview imaginary people. For example, I would say, "Our guest today is Rosemary Clooney," and then I would play her 78-r.p.m. record. Also, during that period, I became obsessed with being a play-by-play sportscaster. So, I would get my bat, a little 78-record with crowd noise, and my new Wilcox-Gay tape recorder and broadcast imaginary baseball games. On every New Year's Day, for at least three or four years, I would set up and call the Cotton Bowl and the Rose Bowl games — I was living this imaginary life of television in my living room.

In those days, I remember going to sleep every night listening to the sounds of radio or television. We had a small apartment, so I could hear the sound coming through the walls into my bedroom. The show that I will never forget was "Life of Riley." Even though I never saw the show, I could hear it. So, I have my own visual description of it. I can also remember going to bed early and and listening to the radio in a little transistor earpiece. I used to lay there listening to baseball games originating from faraway places. One of my earliest television experiences was watching the atomic bomb tests on our Lyon and Healy black and white television. I recall getting up early, in the wee hours of the morning, to watch the tests from Yucca Flats, Nevada.

Every day, I would come home for lunch with Uncle Johnny Coons. I would get home just in time to gobble down a sandwich and sit in front of the television and listen to him say, "Hmm, boy, that looks good!" I remember once when Uncle Johnny said, "What are you boys and girls having for lunch today?" I replied out loud a silly answer and he said, "Hmm, boy, that sounds good!" Of course, I started to laugh. The program was broadcast from the Merchandise Mart every single day from 12:00 to 12:30. When I got home from school, I remember watching "Hawkins Falls" on Channel 5, as well as "Kukla, Fran and Ollie."

Every night, at 5:45, in front of Tribune Tower, they did the show called "The Curbstone Cutup" with Ernie Simon. I used to watch the show, and several times, on more than five occasions, my friend Seymour and I would go down there and try to get on television. If you made it on the show you got a bunch of little goodies, including a box of gift-wrapped Kraft cheese and two tickets to a Balaban and Katz theater. Now, it was a "man-on-the-street" show, and we noticed that whenever it was rainy or inclement, adults would not stick around, so Simon had 15 minutes to fill. So, whenever the weather was bad, we used to take the #76 Diversey bus downtown. We would sort of stand there and wait around, and that's how we got be interviewed by Ernie Simon. I remember once, when Jack Brickhouse was Ernie's substitute, he interviewed me. It was freezing out, and I had cold, rosy cheeks, so he said, "Come on in here!" Well, Jack takes my head and sort of pulls it back, saying, "Get a close-up of this young cherub!" He was doing it playfully, but he was pulling my hair so tight that it made my eyes tear up. So, when they moved in for the close-up I was crying — on WGN-TV!

I would come downtown pretty regularly to see all the different shows that were broadcast from here, including "Petticoat Party" with Frasier Thomas at the Garrick Theater and Robert McCormick's "Chicago Theater of the Air" at the Tribune Tower. I would go to see anything that was happening at WGN. There was a local television show called "Hi Ladies" with Mike Douglas, and I remember him interviewing me once when I was downtown with my mother. He said, "What's your favorite subject?" I said, "Recess." The crowd just roared, and he said, "You're the first kid that's ever been honest with me."

A big television milestone for me came in 1959, when we were one of the first families on the block to get a color television set. We were watching television the night of September 22, 1959, when the White Sox won the American League pennant. We had two televisions on — the color television set was in the front room and we had another little black and white television in the dining room. I was watching the game on the black and white TV, because my mother was holding her regular prayer meeting in the front room. Well, when Vic Power of Cleveland hit into a double play, clinching the pennant for the Sox, I literally let out a war whoop. My mother definitely wanted me to quiet down! It was just so wonderful! I didn't go to a World Series game, but I was listening on the radio. This was in the era when they played the Series' games during the day, so every young boy at Schurz High School had a little transistor radio up to their ear. I was in Mr. Piper's class having a biology test during the first game, and when Ted Kluszewski hit a grand slam home run I was not the only boy in the school to yell out "Yeah!" Luckily, Mr. Piper was hard of hearing, so I don't think he heard us at all.

Bruce DuMont, president of the Museum of Broadcast Communications in Chicago, is the nephew of Allen DuMont, the founder of the DuMont Television Network.

Television in North Side Barber Shop, c.1955
Photograph by William Hugh

Foster Park Memories | Georgie Anne Geyer

I was born in Chicago and lived in Foster Park at 8329 S. Ada Street, which was close to Brainerd and Englewood. It was a nice South Side neighborhood, full of bungalows and lots of trees. I went to Cook Elementary School near 81st and Loomis, and then to Calumet High School near Racine and 81st Street, where I graduated in 1952.

As children and then growing into puberty we loved music, and, in my family, we sang a lot. We had a piano and sang all the songs of the day, and we gave shows a lot, both in Chicago and at our summer home in Lauderdale Lakes, Wisconsin. On Saturday night, at 8 p.m., we would always listen to "Your Hit Parade" on radio. We would make little bets about which songs would be first on the show that week. At Christmas, my serious, hardworking father would play Santa Claus for the family. He was a wonderful Santa, and he would always rent a costume for the occasion.

We had lots of things to do when I was growing up, including roller skating, ice skating, and playing outside. And we did a lot with very little. We played at an empty lot at 83rd Street, which we called the "prairie." We needed a lot of imagination in those years, and kids had their own rules. We would come home from lunch and then go back to school, and we didn't see adults until dinnertime. We were always very busy doing things when we grew up, but we went to those places ourselves because our parents had faith that the city would protect us — and it did. In fact, I took the bus and "L" by myself when I was nine years old. I went to dance lessons and even went downtown alone. There was no fear in those years and our parents didn't worry about us traveling by ourselves. Life was very calm. It was a very serene way of life back then, but the adults were clearly in control. As kids, we never thought of disobeying them. I just remember, like others who were raised in the neighborhood, how happy we were. We would white wash the basement, decorate it and have parties — and think we were in heaven.

When television came out in the late 1940s I was very excited about it. We got a small screen television, and the show I remember then was "Your Show of Shows" with Sid Caesar and Imogene Coca. I don't remember watching much news programming in those days, but the radio was in the kitchen, and that was where we heard the news. I also remember when we got air conditioning in the late 1940s — the little window units — because the bungalows would get very hot in summertime and we often got the odors from the stockyards. That was horrible because the smell was overwhelming! So, I particularly remember the first air conditioners, and we put one in the window of our bungalow living room. The kids next door brought their mattresses over to sleep on the floor in our cool house.

Movies were a big part of my life when I was growing up. The movie theaters that were close to me were the Capital Theater and, if you were really going out, the Southtown Theater. I would go to the movies with both my family or on dates. As for dating, coming from the South Side of Chicago we developed "street smarts." Even though Foster Park was a nice neighborhood, it was a "real" neighborhood. Our mothers would take us aside and tell us, "Now girls, most of the men out there are wonderful, like your fathers and your brothers, but there are also bad men out there, too." So, we learned where to kick long before we knew why.

My family went downtown a lot, and my mother took me to the Harding's Cafeteria on Wabash for lunch, although there were other locations for that restaurant. We also went to other restaurants downtown like Henrici's and Jacque's. We often went out to eat on Sunday to restaurants located further south, like Phil Smidt's.

I became interested in journalism when I was very young. My mother taught me to read when I was four years old because I pushed her to teach me how. I also wanted to write at an early age, so by the time I got to kindergarten, they moved me ahead because I already knew how to read and write. I have been a voracious reader all my life, and, in high school, I just read my way through the library. I would also go to the Chicago Public Library at Halsted and 79th Street. I remember I had to find my own challenges in high school. I was on the school newspaper, but rather than being the editor I had several different positions. I really liked writing rather than editing. I had a column in the paper, and it allowed me to do exactly what I wanted to do.

I graduated from Calumet High School in 1952 and went to Northwestern University in Evanston. I majored in journalism and history and loved it there. I remember the weekend my parents took me to Evanston in the fall of 1952 — I felt that the whole world had opened for me. I discovered that all I had to do was just study and learn.

Georgie Anne Geyer is a nationally syndicated columnist who began her career at the Chicago Daily News.

Bungalows on the Northwest Side, c.1955

Fun in the City

Both Pages: *Residents Open Hydrants on the West Side, c.1955*

Both Pages: *Halloween on the West Side, c.1950*

Both Pages: *Winter on the West Side, c.1950*

Growing Up in Chicagoland | Hillary Rodham Clinton

My parents, Hugh Rodham and Dorothy Howell Rodham, were married in early 1942. During the war, my dad was a chief petty officer at the Great Lakes Naval Training Station where he trained thousands of young sailors before they were shipped out to sea. After the war, he started a small drapery fabric business in the Merchandise Mart called Rodrik Fabrics. I was born in 1947 at Edgewater Hospital, on Ashland near Peterson, and we first lived on Chicago's North Side in the Lincoln Park neighborhood until I was three years old.

In 1950, my father saved enough money to move the family to the northwest suburb of Park Ridge, 18 miles from the Loop. We lived in a two-story, brick house at Elm and Wisner Streets with a screened-in porch and a fenced-in backyard. Park Ridge was a wonderful place to grow up during the '50s. The neighborhood was filled with World War II veterans and their families, and everybody looked out for each other. We were free to go anywhere and we spent as much time outside as we could, like ice skating on the nearby Des Plaines River. I was active as a Brownie and then a Girl Scout, and we often participated in Fourth of July parades, food drives and cookie sales.

The Pickwick Theater at Touhy and Northwest Highway was the main place for my best friend, Betsy Johnson, and me. We would have hamburgers, fries and Cokes at the Pan-Dee's Restaurant next door to the theater, as well as the Robin Hood Restaurant, on Touhy Avenue. We also spent a lot of time at my church, the First United Methodist Church, and could walk there from home. We were usually there a couple of times a week, because in addition to church services, we were there for Sunday School, youth activities, and on Thursday nights, potluck dinner. The library in downtown Park Ridge was also a key place during my childhood. My mother would take me there every week, and during the summer they had a great reading program where, for every book that you read, they would give you a segment of a long worm. If you completed the worm, you got a prize at the end of the summer.

I attended Eugene Field Elementary School in Park Ridge, and I loved it. Field School was only three blocks from my house, so I would come home for lunch everyday. I would always eat, listen to the radio, then go back to school for the rest of the afternoon. I had great teachers there and all the way

through they were so encouraging to me. My sixth grade teacher, Elisabeth King, was especially gifted. She drilled us in grammar and had us writing plays and poetry, and was just an incredible inspiration to me. I remember Field School had a program where you had to be tested on your bicycle-riding abilities before you could ride your bike to school. I practiced and practiced, and when I finally passed the test it was a huge watershed event in my life.

Going to downtown Chicago was a very special occasion when I was young — I would just marvel at the incredible size and beauty of the city. The first time I went to a movie in downtown Chicago was with my grandmother. We went to see the reissue of "The Wizard of Oz" in 1955 — it was an overpowering event. Later, we would go down to see the big 3-D specials and then the wide screen movies. At Christmastime, we would always go down to Marshall Field's and look at the decorations. As I got older and became a teenager, I would go downtown to concerts, the beach or the museums. My favorite museum was the Field Museum, and I just loved going there. The first time I went there was probably in the 4th grade, and it was the first time I ever saw a mummy — it is such a vivid memory. We would often go to the city for field trips when I was in school, so Chicago really was an integral part of my growing up. Even though I didn't actually live in the city, it was so close that it just felt like it was part of my backyard.

When it was time for high school, in 1961, I went to Maine East (then Maine South). It was a huge building, and at first it was very intimidating. At that time, Maine East was one of the largest high schools in the country, with almost 5,000 students. The academics there were great, the extra curricular activities were wide ranging, and the school gave you tremendous opportunities to participate in all sorts of activities. During those years, my high school resembled the movie "Grease" or the popular television program "Happy Days."

Of course, I was in high school when President Kennedy was assassinated, and I learned about it while I was in Mr. Craddock's geometry class. The early '60s was an historic time in our country's history, as well as an important time in my own life. During those years, I became very interested in politics because my father was so interested in the subject. We used to talk about politics over the din-

Cleaning Elephants at the Field Museum, 1958
Photograph by Robert Burley *Chicago Sun-Times*

ner table, and I was a Nixon supporter because my father was a Nixon supporter. At the same time, however, you couldn't help but admire President Kennedy, and, in the aftermath of the assassination, it was a tremendous shock to the national psyche. In the 1964 election my government teacher, Jerry Baker, assigned me to play President Johnson in a mock presidential debate. That assignment forced me to actually learn about Johnson's positions on civil rights, health care, poverty, and foreign policy, and made me consider opinions other than what my father believed. That simple assignment began a real long term change in my own political beliefs.

Hillary Rodham Clinton is a first-term U.S. senator from New York and the former first lady of the United States.

Birth of a Sportsman | Steve Zucker

I was born in 1940 at American Hospital on Irving Park, and my father always told the story of how he had to fill-up a piggy bank, and whatever was in there was the doctor's fee — nobody had money back then. I lived at Rosemont and Western from 1940 until 1950, when we moved to Washtenaw and Granville.

In those years we would ride around on our bicycles a lot. We'd go to places like the Tastee-Freeze on Lincoln Avenue and McDonald's at Peterson and Kedzie, but the most popular drive-in hamburger place in those years was Henry's, on Lincoln near Kedzie. Almost every date I remember going on included going to a movie or miniature golf at Lincoln and Devon. We would also go there for fast pitching batting cages or the go-carts — everything was right there at that location. Later on, in high school, they put up a tent there for dancing on the weekends. When we went out with the guys for movies we would go to the Nortown Theater on Western and Devon, but on dates we would go to the Granada Theater on Sheridan and Devon.

During the summer, we would play softball from the time we woke up until the time it got dark, usually at Green Briar Park. There were no lights at the park, and we had no formal teams or uniforms, so we would play pick-up games of 16-inch softball.

In 1950, I went away to Camp Interlaken, which was owned by Joe Kupcinet, Irv Kupcinet's brother. Everybody talks about Camp Ojibwa, but they couldn't beat Interlaken because we had fabulous athletes there. Sid Luckman, the famous quarterback for the Bears, would come up to camp to see his son, Bobby, who was in the cabin next to me. Sid was great, and he taught me how to grip a football. One of my counselors at the camp was Marv Levy, who later became an NFL coach, and he taught me how to play football. Later in life, after I became a sports agent, I would call the Buffalo Bills to negotiate a contract and Marv would get on the phone — to sing the Camp Interlaken song!

I collected baseball cards and classic comic books in those days. I loved the chewing gum you got with the cards, and that smell of the gum on the cards never leaves you. Of course, my mother threw both of my collections away! I had all the cards from 1948 to 1952, but she threw them out. When I got married in 1970, I took $800 and went to a show at the Holiday Inn and I bought back all the cards, and my wife cried because we didn't have any money at that time. One of the cards was a Mickey Mantle rookie card, and I got the first issue of *Sports Illustrated* at that same time.

My dad had the first television in the neighborhood — an RCA console with a radio, phonograph, and 10-inch screen. It cost $1,000 in 1947, which was a fortune back then. But that was how my dad was, and even though he didn't have that much money he liked to buy certain things. When television came, it changed everything. I would watch whatever I could as soon as I came home from school. There wasn't that much on at that time, but do I remember watching many baseball games. Until there was television I was a big St. Louis Cardinals' fan, but television and Jack Brickhouse changed me into a Cubs fan. All my friends would come over and watch TV because nobody else had one.

Rock and roll began when I started high school in 1954 — so I really grew up with rock and roll. Bill Haley and the Comets were the big stars of the day, where just the year before the popular singers were Patti Page, Rosemary Clooney and Eddie Fisher. Then, all of a sudden, you had Bill Haley and rock and roll — the records were everywhere! We would dance to the music at the assembly hall at school or places that had jukeboxes, like Oddo's Village on Peterson. We would hang out there, or at Allegro's or Papa Milano's. Of course, we always listened to rock and roll on the radio, especially Howard Miller on WIND.

My friends and I started drinking and going to bars when we were about 15 years old, and just doing crazy things. I was totally uninhibited in those days! I didn't study much in high school, but luckily the University of Illinois had to accept you if you graduated from high school. In fact, I was at the University of Illinois for six semesters on probation!

After John Kennedy was elected in November 1960, to celebrate we called up Dean Martin at the Sands Hotel in Las Vegas on a Thursday night. We said to Dean, "We're three guys from the University of Illinois and we want to drive down to Vegas and see your show on Saturday night." So, we spent 36 hours driving to Vegas. When we got there, we met Dean Martin and he put a table on the stage for us. The next day we were sitting there talking and Dean puts his hand on my shoulder and says, "How are you boys getting along? Would you like to fly with me to the wedding of my friend Sammy Davis Jr. tonight in Los Angeles?" We didn't go because we had to get back to school.

Steve Zucker, attorney and sports agent, has represented many of America's most successful athletes, including Jim McMahon, Deion Sanders and Kenny Lofton.

Vote for the 'Orange Man' | Joel Weisman

I was born in 1942, and we moved to West Rogers Park in the early 1950s, where we stayed until I moved out of the house. I had a great time in grammar school and had an active social life. A friend named Arnie Balaban and I put out a newspaper at Rogers Elementary School called *The Social News*. Each week we would rate the popularity of the boys and the girls, and that was where I first learned about the power of the press. Everybody was so nice to me because they were hoping to either be first in our ratings, or move up in our ratings. I also learned the reverse corollary: if we ever dropped somebody down they were furious at us. We were pretty savvy about it because we put ourselves low in the ratings, and then we gradually climbed up. It was just the two of us rating everybody else, and people couldn't wait for our list to come out.

It was an awkward time for most kids at that age, and I remember there would be these parties on Friday nights — kissing parties. We would play "Spin-The-Bottle" and "Post Office," and sometimes we would pass the apple or the orange from person to person — you might get a chin full of someone, or maybe you would feel their body against yours — that kind of stuff. You might have a "date" by picking up someone to go to these parties, and then you would walk them home afterward.

I loved high school. I just couldn't wait to get up in the morning and see all the kids, but my desire had nothing whatsoever to do with learning. I did well, however, and was an officer in the student council and a council representative for a number of years. One year I ran for Treasurer, and I created a campaign slogan that said "Vote for the Orange Man" because I had red hair. I got elected — my first brush with politics. During my years at Sullivan High School they had what were called "social-athletic" clubs, and my club was the Centaurs.

As I think back on it now, it was in some ways a very unfair situation for those who were on the outside of the clubs. It was clearly a caste system of popularity. Those who were in it wanted to be higher in the caste structure, and those who were outside became very resentful and would often crawl into a shell. Interestingly, as the years went by, the club changed from being very limited to very inclusive. By the time we were second-semester seniors at Sullivan we let virtually everyone join the Centaurs — maybe we matured a little bit.

Now, in those days you could go just about anywhere in the city and do anything. There was a feeling of safety in the city and an expectation on the part of the parents that it was good for you to be independent. You could take the bus or the "L" by yourself and they didn't worry about it. My dentist and eye doctor were downtown, so I would travel alone and sometimes, after an appointment, walk around State Street. I had a savings account at Home Federal Savings on Adams and State, and, in those days, I would go to the bank and deposit money from my jobs. Occasionally, I would go see statues around the city, visit the museums, see the Chicago Board of Trade on LaSalle Street, travel to the Garfield Park and Lincoln Park Conservatories — sometimes with friends and sometimes by myself.

I also remember going downtown to the televised dance shows in the '50s, including Jim Lounsberry's show and the "Morris B. Sachs Amateur Hour." For the senior prom, we went downtown to the Black Orchid and for junior prom we took our dates to the Blackhawk Restaurant on Wabash and then saw a movie.

The '50s and early '60s were wonderful years because you really were able to do whatever you wanted to. You see, things back then were not as structured as they are now. If you were a person with any motivation whatsoever, you could learn and experience things, go to all kinds of places, and spontaneously do things you just can't do now — unless you are part of a structured group. There were also a lot of "cultural" things that you learned, not by design, but just by getting around. For example, I would go out to Arlington Park Racetrack with my friend who drove a car. Periodically, we would go out there, pool our money, and the oldest one of us would make the bets. You were supposed to be 18 years old to get in, and we were only 16 at the time. Occasionally, we would go to the harness races at Sportsman's Park as well.

I think kids back then were much more "street-smart" than they are today — much more savvy. As a result, they were quicker studies once they got into the world. It seemed like everybody had some kind of trouble or weakness, but the fear of failing was not as important as it is today. Success was not as simple; there was no such thing as a tried-and-true path to success. We just didn't worry if we had a deviation from the direct path to the top. Expectations of kids and parents were very different during that era. Many parents were Depression-era kids, not as well-educated, or came from large families. As a result, they didn't micromanage their children, and you grew up much quicker than kids do today.

Joel Weisman, lawyer, media agent and award-winning broadcaster, grew up in Albany Park and West Rogers Park.

Happy Days

From poodle skirts to "DAs," many Chicagoans point to the television series "Happy Days" as a close approximation of their years in high school. These photographs of Sullivan High School students seem to provide the evidence, as well as capture the spirit of a city education in the 1950s.

Dating in the Fifties | Sheila Morris Williams

My first dating experiences were at sock hops in the basement of my church, St. Mary's, in Evanston. The priest was always there. He understood that boys and girls wanted to be together, but only under his watchful eye. We were teenagers, so we would just talk and dance — nothing more. I always wore a short-sleeve sweater, wool skirt, bobby socks and gray suede loafers. It would be nice there, with the lights down low, and music from a jukebox. As I got older, I went to school-sponsored proms and holiday dances — those could be quite elegant.

After school, we would all go to Cooley's Cupboard in Evanston for Cokes and fries to "see and be seen." At that time it was very important to be "seen." You would go on a date and hope to be seen because the more dates you had, the more popular you were. Having dates meant that you were attractive, popular and eligible. Back then, girls would date four or five boys at a time. Sometimes it got confusing about who you were going out with — I had to write it all down! These weren't serious relationships, the idea was to just have fun and meet people.

Around this time, I remember going downtown shopping with my friends, and the city would be filled with sailors on leave. They would be everywhere, wearing their "whites" during the summer and their peacoats in the winter. I remember that there would always be 100 sailors sitting on the steps of the Art Institute. They were so young — just starved for attention — and so homesick. Occasionally, we would talk to them, either standing in line for a movie, or getting a Coke at Walgreen's. We also would see them at Riverview Park, and would go on rides with them. It was such an innocent time — you couldn't do this today. We would just visit and flirt with them — and never see them again.

Dating was a different story in those years — there was a strict protocol for dates. A girl would be picked-up at her home — no honking the car and running out — and her date would sit with her parents and prove he was worthy. Unfortunately, many of my dates didn't pass this test, and it could be heartbreaking.

While I was still in high school, I would go to parties that we called "coke-tail" parties — they were called this because they would serve Coke, ginger ale or creme sodas instead of "cocktails." These parties were special because they were usually held before a prom or special dance. Of course, we wore formal clothing — the boys wore tuxedos and the girls wore full-length, full-skirted gowns. I remember going to one in my senior year, and then we all went to the Chez Paree — chaperoned by a few of our parents who hoped to teach us about the adult world of socializing. The club was so glamorous, and after the stage show Jimmy Durante came to our table and sat down with us. He treated us so nicely, and made us feel like adults. I think the experience was a rite of passage for us really — our parents were getting us ready for being out on our own.

After I graduated from high school, my goal was to really try to experience the world. My plan was to move to downtown Chicago, away from Evanston, where everything shut down at 6:30 p.m. I grew up in an Old World home, very conservative, and I wanted to meet people and see some of the world before I settled down. At age 18 most of my friends were getting married. I was totally shocked by this, because I was just getting ready for the world. I had my own plans and ideas, but my friends wanted to get married — some just to get out of their parents' homes. I could not believe it! So, they got married, had children right away, and they never had the chance to experience the city and all it had to offer.

Now, for young ladies, dating in the 1950s was totally different from today. Back then, it wasn't proper for an unescorted woman to go to a downtown restaurant or nightclub in the evening — woman simply were not let in alone, they needed a date. In those days, men used to respect women, and men and women treated each other in a respectful manner. But we still managed to have fun!

When I was 21, I often went out on "sandwich" dates. This when a young woman would have two admirers escort her to a nice restaurant or nightclub — it was more friendly than romantic. I would sit with the two men "sandwiched" between them. The men would be competitive, but only in a gentlemanly way. It was great fun!

After I started working in the Loop at First Federal Savings, I would often go out with my friends for a drink after work. I remember one restaurant where a young man interested in meeting a young lady could have phones sent to both of their tables, then call and talk. Sometimes these calls led to dates, but usually it was just a practice session to fine tune our flirting skills.

I think things changed a lot by the early 1960s. All the innocence that was part of the dating scene was lost, and women were seen in a different light. Men became

much more aggressive, and this was all very shocking to women. I think young women held more power in their relationships in the 1950s — the power of mystery. All of a sudden, this started to change. We were in the midst of a sexual revolution, and we didn't know how to handle it. There were no books written on this subject at the time. It was tremendously overwhelming, and I feel fortunate and grateful to have grown up dur-ing the 1950s. In retrospect, I think I would choose the days of innocence over what girls have to go through today.

Sheila Morris Williams has never strayed far from her Albany Park roots, spending her entire life in the Chicago area.

Above: *High School Students on the North Side, c.1950*

Let's Dance

Both Pages: *Students Dance to Jukebox Music on the North Side, c.1950*

Above: *Dance at Marshall High School, c.1950*

Right: *Dancers at Wedding Reception, c.1950*

Both Pages: *Dance in the Sullivan High School Gymnasium, c.1950*

4 THE SPORTING LIFE

Chicagoans are passionate about their sports, and for children growing up in the 1950s this interest was sparked at a very early age. Both boys and girls played games in the streets, alleys and school yards of their neighborhoods, as well as participated in the organized activities held at local parks, beaches and park district field houses. A love of sports also came from parents, who shared their enthusiasm for athletics by taking kids to professional sporting events and the games they competed in themselves, like softball, bowling or horseshoes.

As children got older, their own favorite teams and players emerged, and it wasn't unusual for kids to attend games on their own — without any parental supervision. Of course, geographic location played a big part in choosing these favorites: White Sox and Cardinals on the South Side and Cubs and Bears on the North Side. No matter how good or bad they are, most Chicagoans have remained true to the teams of their youth, enduring heartbreaking losses or even family moves to a different side of town.

During the '50s, these loyalties would be sorely tested, as fans had to endure much more losing than winning. But from baseball to wrestling and horse racing to midget cars, there was always a lot to cheer about during the decade — win or lose.

The Big Leagues

Things should have been promising for the Cubs in the 1950s, after all, they made it to the World Series in 1945. However, in just three years, the Cubs went from the National League Champions to one of the worst teams in the leagues. In 1948, they were 64-90, in 1949, 61-93, and the team didn't have a winning record again until 1963. These were lean years for the team, but despite the bad records there were many talented and popular Cub players, including Andy Pafko, Hank Sauer and Phil Cavaretta. One player, who came to be known as "Mr. Cub," proved to be a bright light on the North Side: Ernie Banks. His on-field talent earned National League MVP honors in 1958 and 1959, but Chicago fans loved him just as much for his grace and infectious love of the game.

While the Cubs didn't make much history on the field during the era, the television broadcasts of the games did. Beginning in 1948, the groundbreaking coverage on WGN-TV was seen throughout the area, and the innovative ideas employed by Ward Quall, Jack Brickhouse, Jack Rosenberg and Arne Harris still shape the way games are televised today. This coverage, combined with the great radio reporting of Bert Wilson, Milo Hamilton, Jack Quinlan, Charlie Grimm, Vince Lloyd and Lou "The Good Kid" Boudreau, allowed fans to follow the Cubs' exploits no matter where they were. Of course, going to see the games in person was still the preferred choice for most fans, and ticket availability was never a problem in those years. In fact, women could get in free on Tuesday's "Ladies Day" and kids could get in free after the sixth inning.

On the South Side, after a terrible decade in the '40s, the White Sox were assembling a team that would dominate Chicago baseball in the 1950s. Billy Pierce arrived first, followed by Nellie Fox and Luis Aparicio. Soon, all of the components of what would become known as the "Go-Go" Sox were there, including Chico Carrasquel, Minnie Minoso, and Jim Rivera. Under the leadership of General Manager Frank Lane and Manager Al Lopez, the White Sox were strong participants in most of the pennant races of the '50s, but always bowed to the more dominant Yankees or Indians.

Finally, in 1959, after finishing in third place five times during the decade, the Sox won the pennant — their first title since 1919. To celebrate, city officials set off air raid sirens and early the next morning over 100,000 fans welcomed the team home when they returned to Midway Airport. On October 1, the World Series opened at Comiskey Park against the Los Angeles Dodgers, and the Sox got off to a good start with a 11-0 win. Unfortunately, the Sox then lost the next three games in a row, and only managed one more victory before losing the series in six games. The Sox remained competitive in the early 1960s, but were never able to repeat the great success of the 1959 season.

The Chicago Blackhawks, who attracted a small but devoted following to the Stadium each year, struggled for most of the '40s and '50s. During a 13-season span from 1946 through 1958, the Hawks made the NHL playoffs only one time, and for 15 years, from 1946 through 1960, they always had a losing record. It was a highly competitive league in those years, with only six teams compared to today's 30, so the talent level was high — and tough. Players skated without helmets, including the goalies, who now wear elaborate head protection. Things began to look up for the team when they acquired goalie Glenn Hall during the 1957-58 season, and more help was added with players from their junior and minor league teams, including future stars Bobby Hull, Stan Mikita and Pierre Pilote. In 1960-61, the Hawks finally achieved the success the fans were waiting for, beating the Montreal Canadiens in the semifinals and playing against the Detroit Red Wings in the Stanley Cup Championship. As with the White Sox, hopes were high that the talented team would dominate the decade, but despite great individual achievement, like Bobby Hull's record breaking 50-goal season, the Hawks never won another Stanley Cup.

Chicago had two very successful professional football teams during the 1940s, but both struggled during the '50s. The Chicago Cardinals, who played their games at Comiskey Park, won their only NFL Championship in 1947 when they beat the Philadelphia Eagles. Expectations were high in 1948 when they had a chance to make it two in a row, only to lose the championship 7-0 in a rematch with the Eagles. It was downhill from there, as the Cardinals went through four coaches in a six year span, including Green Bay Packer great "Curly" Lambeau, who only lasted ten games. One of the bright spots for the Cardinals was Chicagoan Don Stonesifer, who grew up in the Logan Square neighborhood. "Since my father was a lifelong Bears fan he was quite disappointed I was drafted by the Cardinals," Don remembers, "but he ended up coming to all the Cardinal's games for the next six years. While he fully supported me he would always say, 'I hope you have a good game — except against the Bears!'" The Cardinals had little success in the decade, and in 1959 the team was moved to St. Louis, ending the two NFL team era in Chicago.

Like the Cardinals, the Chicago Bears were also NFL champions during the 1940s, winning in 1940, 1943 and 1946. During the 1950s the team continued to be competitive, and returned to the championship game in 1956, but lost to the Giants by a score of 47-7. It wasn't until the early 1960s, when the Bears drafted Mike Dikta, Bill Brown, Ronnie Bull and Mike Pyle, that the nucleus of their next championship team would be formed. Everything finally came together for the team in 1963, when the Bears beat the New York Giants for the championship.

Wrestlers, Fighters, Bowlers and High Rollers

Wrestling was an extremely popular sport in Chicago, and with the help of heavy television coverage it became even more popular in the 1950s. Athletes with names like "Mighty Atlas," "Tarzan White" and "Lone Eagle" could be found at the area's wrestling venues, including the International Amphitheater, Marigold Arena and the Rainbow Arena. Local promoters used a variety of marketing devices to get people in the seats, like creating feuds and grudges between the wrestlers, and forming specialty leagues, like midget wrestling. "Little Beaver," "Sky Low-Low" and "Pee Wee" James performed in midget tag-team matches, and were known for their speed and agility.

Wrestling coverage on television was among the earliest sports programming in Chicago. WGN-TV began covering the sport in 1948, with Jack Brickhouse hosting a regular program airing Saturday nights at 8:30. Tavern Pale Beer sponsored the show, and in between matches the company would hold the "Miss Tavern Pale" beauty contest, which future television journalist Mike Wallace hosted.

Chicago was a focal point for both amateur and professional boxing in the era, and fights could be seen all around the city. For amateurs, boxing in the annual Golden Gloves Tournament was the highest level, and the competition showcased the city's, as well as the nation's, best fighters. The tournament was created by *Chicago Tribune* sports editor Arch Ward in 1923, and was originally intended for local boxers only. Requests from fighters in other cities quickly forced the competition to expand, and soon regional tournament winners from across the country would bring their champions to Chicago to box. Perhaps the best known winner was Muhammed Ali, then known as Cassius Clay, who won the Golden Gloves heavyweight competition in 1960.

Professional fights were held at a variety of venues around the city, including the Chicago Stadium, Coliseum, International Amphitheater, Soldier Field and Comiskey Park. All the big-name fighters of the era boxed here, like Joe Louis, Ezzard Charles, "Jersey" Joe Wolcott and Rocky Marciano. Major championship fights were held here as well, including the heavyweight championship fight in 1956 when Floyd Patterson knocked out Archie Moore at the Stadium, the welterweight crown in '56 when Johnny Saxton defeated Carmen Basilio, and the middleweight crown in 1957 when "Sugar" Ray Robinson knocked out Jake LaMotta. Unfortunately, as venues in Las Vegas, Atlantic City and international locations became more popular, the number of major championship fights held in Chicago dwindled.

The popularity of bowling in Chicago grew throughout the 1950s, aided in large part by the transition from human pinsetters to automatic pin setting machines. The smaller bowling alleys of the '40s, which catered mostly to men, gave way to larger bowling centers that attracted members of both sexes, some of which even built nurseries for women with small children. Both men's and women's leagues became extremely popular during the decade, and the sight of embroidered bowling shirts, bags and trophies were common in the city and the suburbs. Bowling programs on television helped increase this interest, with many originating from neighborhood locations.

Like bowling, 16-inch softball leagues could be found all over the city, and on many different competitive levels. Kids played the game wherever they could, including prairies, gravel school yards and parking lots. Professional and semi-pro games were played at Bidwell Park and Thillens Stadium — perhaps the mecca for the sport during the decade. Enormous crowds paid to watch the games there on summer nights, with many drawn by the beauty and charm of the park as much as the athletes.

Changing Tastes

Many of the sporting events that were a fixture in the 1950s have totally disappeared from Chicago today. Roller derby matches, bicycle races, midget car races, rodeo competitions and track meets were all held in the city, and though Chicago may seem like an unusual location, events like these could draw a big crowd. A good example of this was the popularity of auto racing, a sport which regularly attracted crowds of 30,000 and once drew 100,000 to a stock car race in Soldier Field.

By the 1960s, however, attendance at many of these events began to dwindle due to changing interests and the increased viewership of televised sports, perhaps the biggest competition. The Negro Leagues, which played at Comiskey Park since 1911, disbanded in 1950. Professional softball at Thillens, a favorite since the late 1930s, took a back seat to little league match-ups by the early 1960s. Even horse racing, a favorite since the 1920s, would see its numbers drop due to off-track betting and legalized gambling.

While the variety of activities may have decreased over the years, the city's passion for sports has always remained constant — even for the losing side — even for Cub fans.

Page 148: *City Football Championship at Soldier Field, c.1950*

At Play

West Side Kids Plot Baseball Strategy, c.1950

Members of the Austin High School Football Team, c.1950

Pick-Up Basketball Game on the Near West Side, 1959

Horseshoe Tournament at Douglas Park, c.1950
Chicago Public Library Special Collections

Veterans of Foreign Wars' Softball Team on the West Side, c.1950

Managers Meet at Ladies Softball Game, Thillens Stadium, c.1950
Thillens Stadium Archive

Rising From the Frozen Tundra of Skokie | Bruce Wolf

My family first lived at Roosevelt and Harding on the West Side before we moved to Skokie in the late 1950s, where we lived in a couple of different places. When I was growing up we would ride our bikes to McNally Park, right next to Middleton School, across the street from the Rand McNally Company. There was also a series of kiddie parks in Skokie, one of them called Navaho Park, where huge numbers of kids would play wiffle ball everyday for hours on end during the summer. You would go out in the early morning and wouldn't come home until late in the day in those days — there was nothing to keep you in the house during the summer.

My earliest sports memories include being taken to a Cubs' game at Wrigley Field when I was about five years old. We were sitting very close to the field, and to see the batters swinging their bats up close was mind-boggling to me! The one thing that I remember most of all was that the scoreboard in center field looked like it was miles and miles away. From the perspective of a five-year-old, it had to look really far away. I don't remember going to another game for a number of years, but the next time I went to Wrigley Field I was on my own, which we used to be able to do all the time. I remember telling everybody ahead of time, "Wait until you get to see this because the scoreboard is miles and miles away." Well, by this time I was 10 years old, and the scoreboard looked like it was right in my lap. So, the perspective had totally changed.

In order to go to the games, we would take the No. 9 or No. 10 Evanston bus to the Howard "L" and then get off at Addison for Wrigley Field. Once I went to Wrigley with a friend named Larry Hoke for a doubleheader in the middle of the week, and the upper grandstand had nothing but seats available. We were sitting up there, just to the left of home plate in the second tier of the upper deck, even though there was almost nobody else around. Larry had a Frosty Malt, and he took the top of the lid and threw it like a Frisbee. It landed right over the WGN-TV camera that was located in the basket behind home plate, just below the upper deck. An Andy Frain usher came by because we were the only ones there, and he asked, "Which one of you guys did that?" We looked at each other and said to him, "We didn't do it." So, he didn't throw us out of the ballpark, even though it was a perfect Frisbee throw.

I had a strong interest in hockey because in 1961 the Blackhawks won the Stanley Cup. Bobby Hull, Stan Mikita, Glenn Hall, and all the big names are from that era, when hockey ruled in Chicago. I was probably about nine or ten years old when I went to my first hockey game with my father, and later he wound up becoming a Blackhawks' season ticket holder, so we went to lots and lots of games. In the early 1960s I only went to a few games, but I would watch them all the time at home on WGN-TV with Lloyd Pettit as the announcer. I loved watching the Blackhawks on WGN, and I would watch every single game I possibly could. I was a diehard Blackhawk fan and I knew all the players, and I still know all the uniform numbers of the great Blackhawks of the 1960s and 1970s, including No. 3 Pierre Pilote, No. 4 Moose Vasco, No. 5 Matt Ravlich, No. 6 Reggie Fleming, No. 7 Pit Martin, and all three of Bobby Hull's jersey numbers, 16, 7 and 9.

I remember watching the Blackhawks in a playoff game and my father and I were really excited because it was an overtime game. He was smoking a cigarette while we were watching, and I think that Mikita scored an overtime goal and the Blackhawks won the game. My father got so excited he threw the cigarette up in the air and didn't see where it went. We were looking around for it when, all of a sudden, he realized that the lit cigarette landed in his hair after hitting the ceiling!

In those years it was really difficult to get a ticket to a Bears game at Wrigley Field. In fact, when I was ten years old the Bears played in the NFL Championship game and even that was "blacked out" in Chicago. We had to go to Rockton, Illinois at the Wagon Wheel Resort to see the game on television. In those days, you could fiddle with your "rabbit ears" antenna on your television to try to pick up the Bears on a South Bend television station, but in 1963 we had to go through a real ordeal just to see the championship game. So, we made a vacation out of it at the Wagon Wheel in Rockton. I remember being in a smoke-filled room with a little black and white television. Since I was a 10-year-old kid I didn't have a good position in the room, so I could barely see over men's heads. I do remember seeing Richie Petitbone intercept a pass — it was wild and everyone was going nuts over the play! It was exciting just to be there, even though I barely saw any of the action.

Bruce Wolf attended Northwestern University and Chicago Kent School of Law before a career in sports reporting on WXRT, WLUP and Fox-TV.

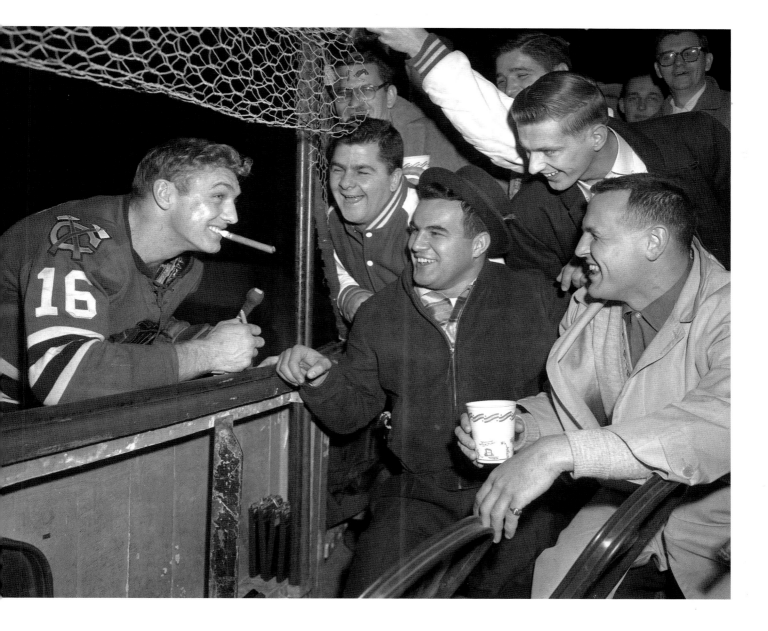

Bobby Hull Meets His Fans, 1959
Photograph by Merrill Palmer *Chicago Sun-Times*

'The Boy Wonder' | Carmen Salvino

I was born in 1933 and lived on Chicago's West Side at Flournoy and Ashland. We moved back and forth to Florida when I was a kid, but finally came back to the city for good when I was about twelve years old. It was about that time when I started setting pins at a bowling center, which was how I got my start in bowling. Someone told me that I could make $1.50 a night at the Amalgamated Center, a clothing union, located on Ashland and Van Buren. The lanes were located in the basement of the building, and I set pins there for three or four years before I started bowling in a league. I was about 15 years old when I bowled in my first league and I had a 164 average — a year later my average increased to 193. At 17, I was averaging 200 while I was still at Crane Technical High School. One of the good teams in Chicago asked me to bowl with them in the ABC Tournament in Minnesota, but I had to get permission from my high school principal to get out of school. I went to the tournament and shot a 699 series in the singles and almost won the event. After that, some of the best teams in Chicago picked me up and soon I was bowling in the Chicago Classic League.

I guess I was what they called a "phenom." At 17, I was bowling in a professional league — that is, and was, unheard of in the sport. It usually took guys until their late '20s before they became great. This created a lot of problems when I was a kid, particularly from older men who resented me. They made a lot of remarks, which caused me to become very cocky. I got a big chip on my shoulder and became known as the "cocky punk from Chicago." I didn't really get any guidance from my mother and father at the time, so my only way to defend myself was with my hands and my mouth. I don't regret growing up that way because I think it toughened me up and made me a better bowler. Every time they would try to knock me, I would just work that much harder to whip them. And I did whip them, because by the time I was 19 years old I was the best bowler in the City of Chicago, and was named the "Boy Wonder."

It wasn't long before a bigger team wanted to pick me up, so I bowled with a team that included Joe Norris and Joe Wilman — who was 41 years old at the time. We bowled against Don Carter and Fred Bujack in 1953, and Joe Wilman and I won the National Match Game Doubles Championship. I remember sitting on the bench when I was bowling with Wilman and saying to myself, "I hope this old guy don't conk out on me!" That's ironic, because years later I had

a similar incident happen to me when I was bowling a tournament in Arizona. I was averaging about 241 for the six games, and the kid I was bowling against was only about 24 years old — and I was 51 years old. He calls me to the side and said, "Do you mind if I ask you a question, Mr. Salvino?" I already knew I was in trouble. He said to me, "How old are you?" I said to him, "Kid, back up a little bit. I don't want my bowling ball to hear me. I'm 51 years old, but as long as that ball doesn't know I'm all right and it will keep striking!"

Bowling with Wilman and Norris was a very good experience for me when I was young. I traveled with them throughout the country, and they gave me something I needed at the time — adult guidance — because I was ready to strike back at everybody! My first big tournament victory came in 1952 when I won the Dom Devito Classic, held on Chicago's South Side against 3,000 bowlers from all over the country. I think I created a lot of resentment with that win, as well as other wins I got at a very young age.

One time, Ray Bluth, a Hall of Fame bowler from St. Louis, tried to psyche me out during a tournament. I was bowling in an all-star tournament and he started coughing in time with my feet as I was going to the line. Since I was still a rookie, and my concentration wasn't strong yet, I heard him quite clearly. The next game he was coughing faster, and my feet were going faster! As soon as there was a break in the action I put my finger in his face and said, "If you cough one more time, I'm going to put your lights out." That was the only way I knew how to defend myself. He was a very nice guy, and his response was calm and cool, "If you hit me, I'll sue you." I said to him, "You cough one more time and you're not going to get a shot at suing me — I'm going to put your lights out!" So, I got up to bowl and there was no cough, but now I couldn't start my steps. I was saying to myself, "Come on, give me one little cough to get me started!" He didn't cough, however, so I had to readjust my rhythm, and then I beat him the next two games. As we were leaving I put my arm around Ray and said, "Ray, you owe me for a doctor's bill." He said, "What are you talking about?" I said, "I cured your cough." About 30 years later, we met at the Legends of Bowling, but before I got there I went to the drugstore and bought a box of cough drops. When I saw him I gave him the drops and said, "Nothing has changed. Take those cough drops now because if you cough I'm still going to put your lights out!

Bowling was big in Chicago during the 1950s, and a lot of great bowlers came out of here, including Buddy Bomar, Paul Krumske, Ned Day, Joe Kristof and many other great ones, too. I remember that in the '50s there was a popular bowling show in Chicago with "Whispering" Joe Wilson as the announcer. They broadcast live bowling matches on television from the Faetz and Niesen Bowling Lanes on Ridge at Clark, on the Far North Side. Joe Wilson was such a nice man, and he once invited all of us to his home in Wilmette. I really enjoyed being around him.

Of course, the sport is a lot different today than it was in the '50s and '60s, but I like the way the Professional Bowlers Association is running things now — with more action in the tournaments and more one-on-one action. When I first learned to bowl, we bowled on shellac bowling lane surfaces, so that you didn't have to throw the ball too hard. Then, a transition was made to lacquer surfaces, and you could throw the bowling ball a little harder. So, as the surfaces and the materials used to make bowling balls have changed, we've had to change our style and technique as the game evolved. In a way, most athletes are environmental champions, adapting to the materials and surfaces used, just like Astroturf in baseball and football. So, it is not only an athlete's age that is important, but it's also the ability to adapt to changes in a sport. I believe that in any sport an athlete has to rely on the mind and body, and I have sought to develop my mind over my years by learning physics and chemistry.

One of my biggest competitors over the years has been Dick Weber. Not only is he a great bowler, but he's also a great ambassador for the sport. To this day, we still tease each other, and just recently he was on the History Channel. After the show I called him up and said, "Man, you looked pasty on the show — like a ghost. You ought to start wearing makeup when you are on television." He said, "Well, you don't look so hot yourself now that you are a little older." So, Christmas came and I received a package from St. Louis, and my wife and I were wondering who had sent it. It turned out to be a makeup kit from Dick Weber — including rouge, nail polish and lipstick.

Carmen Salvino, Hall of Fame bowler and lifelong Chicagoan, is still competing in tournaments around the country.

Carmen Salvino, c.1955
Chicagoland Sports Hall of Fame

Chicken Wings and Knuckle Sandwiches

Above: *Mighty Atlas vs. Lou Thesz, International Amphitheater, 1951*

Top Right: *Nature Boy Buddy Rogers vs. Rudy Kay at the Madison AC Arena, 1950*

Bottom Right: *Frankie Talabel vs. Ivan Rasputin at the Rainbo Arena, 1950*

Above: *Women Wrestlers at the Rainbo Arena, 1955*

Right: *Antonio Rocca (on floor), Jim Londos (left) and Ali Baba, "The Terrible Turk," at Postls Gym, 1950*

Midget Racing

Midget car racing was a popular spectator sport in the 1950s, with big crowds attending races at Soldier Field, Raceway Park and the Chicago Coliseum. The cars were fast and agile, and drivers took great pride in their construction and engineering. Racers from around the nation competed here, the winners collecting purses that were among the largest in the country.   Robert Middaugh Collection

Chicago's 'Field of Dreams' | Mel Thillens, Jr.

Softball was a big deal at Thillens Stadium in the 1940s, and all over the city. It was pre-television in those days, and big crowds would come out to the park at night. In fact, we had lights at the park in 1940. I've always said: we are the oldest lit baseball park in the city. We had 5000 people out there watching men's 16-inch softball in those days — and these were serious games. We used to have jackpot games for $500.00, but that was nothing compared to what the players had going on. There was a lot of gambling going on in the stands as well.

Throughout the 1940s there were good-sized crowds at the stadium, and we had men's and women's softball, as well as women's baseball. Things began to change in the late 1940s though — the crowds weren't as big — that's when we started Little League. At first, my father saw it as a good opening act for the other games. He put out a call for tryouts and over 10,000 kids showed up. Over 10,000 kids! He hired professional and college coaches to whittle this group down to four teams, and they would play in the preliminary games before our nightly softball games. These kids were good. In 1951, we went to Williamsport, Pennsylvania, for the Little League championship and came in third, and in 1952, we came in second. Things changed after that because Little League then added boundary rules, which meant we couldn't draw kids from all over the city.

So, we dropped out of Little League and changed the name to Thillens Boys Major League. We grew from having just the four original teams to a league with over 1100 kids and 17 paid coaches, managers, assistant managers and so on. These weren't volunteer fathers, they were all professionals. By the early 1950s men's and women's softball started to fade out at our park and the Boys Major League took over. It just kept growing and growing. We had kids coming from all over the area to participate. Even future Mayor Richard M. Daley played at Thillens when he was a kid, back around 1955.

Our boy's league was just like the Major Leagues, including exact replicas of the Major League uniforms — the cost of the uniform was the same, too! They were made by Wilson, the same company that made the pro's uniforms — and the games were broadcast on WGN-TV with Arne Harris working as the cameraman. Jack Brickhouse credited the most famous camera shot in baseball — the shot from behind the pitcher — as being developed at Thillens Stadium.

We also had promotions at Thillens that rivaled the Major Leagues, and we were constantly doing things at the park. We had the Miss Luxembourg beauty contest, donkey baseball, "The King and his Court" and "The Queen and her Court."

"The King," Eddie Feiner, started coming to Thillens in 1946, when he would put on a show and pass the hat for money. He was quite a performer, and he would put on a show similar to what the Harlem Globetrotters would do. Eddie was a incredible pitcher, and he would take on any nine-man team with just four guys on his team. That's right, a nine-man team against his four-man team. He had himself, a catcher, a first baseman and a shortstop. He was just a phenomenal pitcher, and his team would rarely lose. He used to say, "I don't think I'm the best pitcher in the world, I just don't think there's anybody better than me." And he was right! His fastball was clocked at 104 mph, and he had curves and sinkers, too.

I once saw him strike out a guy pitching from the centerfield fence on three pitches. He actually threw that ball aiming at the left field stands — it would break right around shortstop and then float in for a strike. The guy just stood there, he could not figure out when to swing at the thing. Eddie would pitch more games in a year than most guys in a career, and drive 300 miles to get to them.

I remember one game when the opposing team would not go along with Feiner's routines. Then, in about the third inning, he backed off the mound and said, "You want a ball game? You got one!" He did not waste one pitch over the next twelve batters — he fanned every man on three pitches — boom, boom, boom. And these were good players!

Thillens Boys Major Leagues ended in 1964, but we still rent out the park for games all summer long. And I continue to get letters from people who played in our league as kids. In fact, I've called on customers, who after I've introduced myself, will say, "Thillens! I remember my championship game in 1957, there were runners on first and third...." They were reliving a big game from their childhood right there! I've also had mothers come up to me and tell me that they aren't going to let their kids play at the park anymore because they couldn't get them to sleep the night before — the kids were too excited!

We've had four generations now play at the field. Great-grandfathers watching their great-grandchildren. One of our former groundskeepers once said to me, "This is the closest a lot of these kids will ever get to playing at a Major League Park." And it's true — this is their "Field of Dreams."

Mel Thillens, Jr. is president of the Thillens Stadium Foundation, a non-profit organization that operates the North Side ballpark.

Mother's Day at Thillens Stadium, c.1950
Thillens Stadium Archive

Building an NHL Champion | Harvey Wittenberg

I started going to Blackhawk games on a regular basis in the early 1950s. In those years, the Blackhawks were the cellar-dwellers of the six-team National Hockey League, and they didn't make the playoffs too often. In the 1952-53 season, with a bunch of old veterans that nobody really wanted, they finished in fourth place to make the playoffs. Unfortunately, they took on the Montreal Canadiens, the "New York Yankees" of the the National Hockey League.

In that series, the Hawks were on the verge of up-setting the Montreal Canadiens. Al Rollins was the Blackhawk goalie, and he was very good, but he had no defense to help him. He virtually kept them in the playoffs. Montreal won the first two games, Chicago eked out a couple of victories in the next two games, and then the series went back to Montreal. The Hawks won the game and were leading the series 3-2 going back to Chicago, and were on the verge of one of the biggest upsets at that time in NHL history. I'll never forget the opening face-off — Blackhawk Jimmy Mc-Fadden skated past Doug Harvey, one of the all-time great defensemen, and came in pointblank on Jacques Plante. Plante kicked the shot out, and Montreal went on to win the game 3-0. The series then went back to Montreal, who wound up winning in seven games. After that, the Hawks didn't make the playoffs again for another six years in the '50s.

A major change came when Arthur Wirtz and James D. Norris purchased the Blackhawks in 1954. Jim Norris was really the sportsman and Arthur Wirtz was more of the financial guy. The Norris family and the Wirtz' owned Madison Square Garden in New York, the St. Louis Arena, the Chicago Stadium, and Norris' brother owned the Detroit team. So, they actually had control of three of the six teams in the NHL.

When Wirtz and Norris took over, they started to rebuild the team. They hired Tommy Ivan as general manager, who was the coach of the Detroit Red Wings, and had led Detroit to four first-place finishes and two Stanley Cups. The team struggled, and there were a series of coaches that Ivan hired and fired because the team was just doing terribly. The Hawks didn't even have a farm system until Ivan came on board! During those years, the Chicago Stadium was pretty empty. In fact, I remember going to a game against the Bruins and there only about 1,500 fans in attendance — they had to pull people in off the street.

In 1957, Tommy Ivan made a trade with the Detroit Red Wings to get Glenn Hall as goalie, and that was

when the Blackhawk franchise started turning around. In those days, teams only had one goalie — the assistant trainer on the team was the backup goalie — and Glenn Hall went on to set the record by starting 503 consecutive regular season games in goal. He used to throw up before every game — goalies are a breed unto themselves! When Glenn Hall played for the Hawks he never wore a mask, and he never came to training camp because he played every game during the 70-game season — he just didn't want to go through all the rigors of playing in exhibition games. Next, Bobby Hull and Stan Mikita came up from the juniors, as well as Pierre Pilote, who had toiled in the minors in Buffalo. Pilote was a very popular player, and he was clearly ahead of his time as an offensive-minded defensive player. In those days, the defensemen never led offensive rushes, and Doug Harvey of the Canadiens was the best all-around defenseman of his time. Pilote was the first defenseman, outside of Doug Harvey, who moved up on the play. As a fan, I had a clear sense in 1957 that the team was turning around — they had made it back to the playoffs.

I remember one playoff game in April 1959, two years before they won the Stanley Cup. They were playing the Montreal Canadiens in the semifinals and the referee was "Red" Storey, who was an old-time, classic referee. The Hawks lost the game 5-4, and there was a riot after the game. Litzenberger of the Blackhawks got tripped in the open ice and Montreal got the puck away from him, but the referee didn't call a penalty and then Montreal went down the ice and scored. This had happened on three different occasions to three different Hawks, and Montreal went on to win the Stanley Cup. The fans were so upset that they came out on the ice, one with a chair to hit the referee over the head and Doug Harvey hit the fan with a stick. Another fan tried to pour a cup of beer over the referee's head. After the game, they asked Clarence Campbell, the president of the NHL, who was at the game, what happened with Red Storey's officiating. Campbell was quoted in the press as saying, "Apparently, he choked." Because of Campbell's nonsupport, Storey resigned from hockey and never refereed another game in the NHL. Later in life, Storey was asked what happened and his response was, "I felt that I should let the players play the game." But there were three definite situations where penalties could have been called which led directly to Montreal goals, and they wound up winning the game, the series, and, later, the Stanley Cup.

In the 1960-61 season, the Blackhawks won the Stanley Cup. The Hawks finished in third place in the season standings, so they were matched against the first place team, the Montreal Canadiens, and beat them. The Hawks then faced Detroit and beat them four games to two — and won the Stanley Cup. It was a great series, and the Hawks should have won at least three or four Stanley Cups in the '60s. I've talked to Pierre Pilote, Glenn Hall, Bill Hay, Eric Nesterenko, Stan Mikita and Bobby Hull — they all felt that they should have won several times during those years. I guess that it was just the "breaks of the game" that they didn't win any more Stanley Cups.

They had some great talent in those years — Hull and Mikita were the greatest one-two punch in the league. Both of them won the scoring title and the Hart Trophy for Most Valuable Player, and Mikita set a record that has never been equaled: he won all three major trophies in one season — scoring, MVP, and Lady Byng for Most Sportsmanlike — two years in row. No one else has ever won three trophies in one season, including guys like Wayne Gretzky and Mario Lemieux. Pound for pound, Mikita was the best player, while Hull was the most exciting player. Scotty Bowman, who is the all-time winning coach in the NHL with various teams, says that Glenn Hall was the best goalie who ever played for him. Today, Mikita, Hull, Pilote, and Hall are all in the Hockey Hall of Fame.

There were some great games played at the old Chicago Stadium — the building literally shook when the fans were roaring there. Keith Magnuson once told me that when he signed out of the University of Denver to play for the Blackhawks his agent said, "The first time you play in the Chicago Stadium, you'll never hear anything like it in your life." But Keith didn't know what he was talking about. Well, his agent got it right, because Keith told me, "Yes, the first time I came up the stairs from the locker room I heard that roar from the crowd. I never heard anything like it in my life." The thing about the old Chicago Stadium was not only the sound, but the rink was actually smaller than the official dimensions of an NHL rink. So, for the visiting team, it was a very tough building to play in, because the fans were so much closer to the action.

Harvey Wittenberg spent 40 years as the Blackhawk's public address announcer at Chicago Stadium. He is the author of Tales of the Chicago Blackhawks.

Above: *"Hawks on Ice," 1950*
Chicago Sun-Times

Bearing Down in Chicago | Johnny Morris

I grew up in Southern California and graduated from the University of California-Santa Barbara. I was hoping to be drafted into professional football, but I wanted to play in the Los Angeles area. The last place I wanted to go was Chicago, since I had never been out of California. But after I was drafted it didn't take me long to realize that Chicago was a much better place than California.

My first year with the Bears was in 1958. I was just a 22 year-old kid and I was awed by the big city. I'll never forget when I arrived at training camp, they had all the rookies come to Soldier Field to get on a bus to ride to Rensselaer, Indiana. I remember that George Halas showed up at the bus. He said, "I want to welcome you guys." In those days he was kind of like the God of professional football. We were in awe that he had come over to the bus and welcomed us.

Playing for George Halas was a unique experience, because he was the coach, the general manager and the owner — you dealt with him on all three levels. So, it was a tough situation to go in and deal with contract issues with him while, at the same time, you were playing for him as the coach. Of course, in those years, the players didn't have any bargaining power, and he refused to deal with agents. We would have to go one-on-one with him for salary, and I don't think that any of us liked the salaries that we were offered. There was no free agency in those days and they could trade you anytime they wanted to do it. You made a good living, but you didn't get rich playing pro football, especially for the Bears. I have no complaints, but there were some guys who never really got ahead financially because Mr. Halas was pretty tight with his money. Like Mike Ditka said, "Halas threw nickels around like manhole covers." But, he had a lot of good points about him, too.

They drafted me as a running back/halfback, and I played three years at the running back position. Up until that time, most of the ends and wide receivers were big, tall, and slower guys. Then came the thinking: what about putting limber, quicker guys out there as wide receivers and flankers? I think that the first players that they really tried that with were Bobby Mitchell, Tommy McDonald and myself. We were really the first three guys, who were little guys, who were put out there as wide receivers, and it really started a trend. Of course, it helped me a lot because I was only 5'10" and 180 lb., and playing as a running back I probably wouldn't have lasted nearly as long. So, in 1961, I moved to wide receiver and played the rest of my career at that position.

As for playing at Wrigley Field — I loved playing there. During my years with the Bears, we played our exhibition games at Soldier Field, but we played our regular season games at Wrigley Field. I liked Wrigley Field a lot better because it was more "homey." I remember getting knocked out of bounds on a lot of passes at Wrigley Field, and while getting up I'd always see the same fans in the stands every week. After I retired the Bears played all their games at Soldier Field, and it just wasn't the same tradition as it was at Wrigley Field. The end zones at Wrigley were very short, and I think that the south end zone was only about eight yards deep on the east half, so you had the wall about a foot beyond it. I'm surprised that more people didn't get hurt from that. And the goal posts were right on the goal line, too! In fact, I remember when a guy ran full speed into the post — somebody from Detroit — and I thought that he was never going to get up, but he did.

After I was done with football, my challenge was to do well in television. Beginning in 1960, it became very popular to see athletes talking about the games they had just played in. One of the first was CBS in New York who hired Frank Gifford and Pat Summerall to come down on Sundays after the game. So, the general manager of CBS in New York called the general manager of their station here and said, "You know what? This has really gone over good. You should get an athlete on television in Chicago to talk about the Bears."

They ended up contacting me, and inquired whether I could be on WBBM on Sunday nights. I thought about whether I should ask Mr. Halas if I could do this, but I knew he'd say "no" if I asked him. Everything that I had ever asked him, his first answer was always "no." So, I decided not to ask him, and I just went on television one Sunday night. Do you know something? He never said anything to me about it, so I just kept doing it. He never said a word. I was so shocked, and maybe it was because I went ahead and did it without asking him — maybe he respected that — just like Mike Ditka. Mike was always in trouble with Halas, and he ended up trading Ditka. Yet, 20 years later, Halas hired Mike as the head coach of the Bears, so he must have respected him. Maybe that was why he didn't call me in and "chew" me out, because I never bothered to ask him. I went ahead and did it on my own.

Johnny Morris still holds the Bears' record for career receiving yards (5059).

Johnny Morris and Rummie Lound, 1958
Photograph by Joe Kordick *Chicago Sun-Times*

Remembering Football at Comiskey Park | Phil Bouzeos

In 1947, I took over as the assistant equipment manager for the Chicago Cardinals. My days with the team were fantastic, and I stayed with the team until 1958, the year before they moved to St. Louis. The Cardinals played in Comiskey Park, except in 1958, when they played in Soldier Field. The team had a core of 10,000 fans, while the Bears had a core of 20,000-25,000 fans — Chicago was always a Bears town, just like the Cubs.

The players weren't paid big salaries in the 1950s, and one time I was passing out the checks to the players and I asked Tom Wham, a defensive end, "Where are you going after practice?" He said, "I'm going downstairs to cash my check at the newspaper stand." That's how small the checks were. Most of the players felt that if they could just get through the season and end up buying a new car for about $1,500 it would be a great year for them.

The Cardinals should've had a dynasty after the 1947 Championship team. In fact, in 1948, they had a better ball club. At the beginning of the season, however, their star tackle, Stan Mauldin, had a heart attack at Comiskey Park after we played the Philadelphia Eagles. He died about an hour and a half after he left the game. We did have a good season despite the loss, and we did go to Philadelphia to play against them for the championship, but we lost 7-0.

In 1950, Curly Lambeau became the head coach of the Cardinals after being the founder and head coach of the Green Bay Packers. He had a great record with the Packers, but they had a few bad years, too, so he came to the Cardinals. He was the head coach for a year and a half — they fired him halfway through his second year.

The first year he was with the Cardinals, on the first day of practice, he came up to me and said, "Phil, I have to go set up my apartment downtown. Watch over things." Well, before I knew it everybody disappeared and went up to Waukegan and North Chicago. The next morning, I woke up with four or five scantily-clad women running around at the training camp!

During the 1950s the team struggled. I think we had a pretty good team, but we ended up second in our division. Joe Stydahar was the coach, but he never recovered from being fired by the Los Angeles Rams. The man who should have taken over as general manager of the Cardinals was Stormy Bidwell.

Instead, Walter Wofner, who was married to Violet Bidwell, took over, and though he was nice to me, he wasn't a great general manager — that began the decline of the Cardinals. It seemed to me that they never had a chance in Chicago because of the Bears. I didn't like the Bears at that time, naturally, and since I am Greek, I used to tell the guys before we played the Bears that if we beat them, I would pay for a lamb dinner. So, every time we beat the Bears I would buy the lunch — and we used to beat them all the time. The greatest experience ever was when all the Bears had to do was to beat the Cardinals and they would win the division championship in 1955. Well, we played them at Comiskey Park and beat them 53-14. Ollie Matson, Don Stonesifer and Dave Mann all had a couple of touchdowns, and we had a party that lasted a day and a half. It was a great rivalry between the Cardinals and the Bears, and there was no love lost between the two teams. The Cardinals would play the Bears twice a year, home and home, and we averaged 50,000 fans a game — no matter where we played. It was the biggest sports rivalry in the city and would have continued if the Cardinals hadn't moved to St. Louis. The way that professional football was starting to become so popular, there was no reason that Chicago couldn't support two football teams.

We had some interesting players in those years. George Berndt, a tackle, was one of the first 300 lb. players in the NFL. Most of the ballplayers of the '50s weighed 250 pounds as tackles, and if you weighed more you were considered to be fat. Well, George knew that he wasn't going to make the team, so he came up to me on a Saturday and he said, "Phil, if I get cut, don't tell me that I've been released. On Sunday morning, I want one more shot at the Sunday afternoon meal!" Another time, we had a tailor for the team, Larry Gersh, who had a store on Jackson Boulevard and made the clothes for all the players. He said to me, "Phil, I've got a problem because a lot of the rookies signed up for suits from me." I told him, "Don't do anything. I'll let you know who made the team. If they make the team, I'll let you know and you can finish their suits. If they don't make the team, stall them off because they won't have any money to pay you." So, the rookies would come up to him and say, "When is my suit going to be ready." He would say, "Sorry, it's still on the cutting block."

Coach Ray Richardson of the Chicago
Cardinals at Comiskey Park, 1955
Photograph by Mickey Rito *Chicago Sun-Times*

The guy who really made the Cardinals great in those years was Elmer Angsman. He was probably the greatest person whom I ever met in pro sports. Elmer played at Mt. Carmel and then went to Notre Dame. In college, Elmer played a lot, and in a game against Navy he got hit without a mouthpiece and lost 12 teeth. He still holds the rushing record for the NFL championship game because he averaged 15.5 yards per carry against Philadelphia. The Eagles were playing an eight-man line, and if Elmer got beyond the line of scrimmage he could run forever. In fact, he had two runs of 75 yards each. There were four touchdowns that day in Chicago and the Cardinals won the 1947 NFL Championship 28-21.

Phil Bouzeos served as equipment manager of the Cardinals until the team moved to St. Louis in 1959.

Meeting Mr. Wrigley | Jim Brosnan

I was born in 1929 and grew up in Cincinnati, Ohio. I became interested in baseball from the time I was eight years old, when I played on a team in the Knot-Hole League, the precursor of Little League. At the age of 18, I pitched for the American Legion of Cincinnati and we went to the National Championships in South Carolina, where the Midwest scout for the Chicago Cubs saw me. He was responsible for me signing my first contract in professional baseball in 1947. I got a bonus to sign a contract for $2,500. Today, if you are a first round draft choice, you get at least $1,000,000.

My first team was in Elizabeth, Tennessee, playing Class D baseball. A lot of minor league ballplayers used to end up in Class D baseball, and then their careers were over — you couldn't get any lower than that in professional baseball. I played there and had a good year, winning 17 games. After that, I bounced around a bit, playing Class AAA with the Los Angeles Angels, a AAA team in Springfield, Massachusetts, a AA team in Nashville, a Class A in Des Moines, Iowa, and, finally, in Decatur. My year was very bad, and I kept on being moved to lower level farm teams. I didn't think of quitting baseball, but I did think that they were going to forget about me. In 1950, I got my notice to report to the Army, so I figured that it would probably do it for my career after spending four years in the Cubs' minor league system.

When I reported to Ft. Meade, Maryland, the sergeant who was in charge told me two things: first, get to know the master sergeant who paid you, and second, if they asked whether any of us had played national sports, raise your hand — maybe raise both hands! So, I raised both hands and I ended up playing baseball in the Army. My record was 32-2, with one of those losses to New York Yankee pitcher Bob Turley, who was at an Air Force base in Texas. The other game I lost was to Johnny Antonelli, who pitched for several big league teams.

I got out of the Army in 1953 and went back to the Springfield, Massachusetts, team. About that time, I decided that I had had enough of the Cubs' organization, so I went to school in Washington, D.C. on the GI Bill to learn accounting. I had taken one of those interest inventories in the military and was matched best with being either a journalist or an accountant. Since I knew that journalists never made any money, I thought it would be best if I went to the accounting school. Well, not long after that I got a letter from the Cubs asking me to come to spring training. I couldn't believe that I was being invited to spring training after a 4-17 record my last year in the minors, until I saw that that two of the other guys had records as bad as mine.

So, I went to spring training. I had gone into the Army weighing 180 pounds but came out weighing 230 pounds. Now, one of things you do a lot as a pitcher in spring training is run from sideline to sideline — at least ten times just to warm up, and then another ten times at the middle of the day and ten times when you finish. It soon became clear that I wasn't in shape, and one of the coaches, Stan Hack, said, "It shows that you are laboring out there." So, of course, I had to run another ten times. I may not have been in good shape, but I could throw the baseball. One of my minor league managers once said to me, "You seem to be giving us more trouble than you're worth, but you have an arm, and we prize arms. We see a kid with a good arm and we'll do anything we can to develop the kid." Well, I had the arm, and the arm was working, so I made the team.

In 1954, I started the year in Chicago but only lasted until about mid-July, when they sent me back to the minors in Beaumont, Texas. When I landed in Texas the temperature was 104 degrees. For the next 14 days, it got over 100 degrees every day and I lost 14 pounds. I was losing a pound a day, and I didn't know what I was going to look like by the time the season was over!

In 1955, I thought I had made the Cubs during spring training, but was kind of shocked when I learned that I was going to start the season in Los Angeles with the Angels back in AAA baseball. I spent all of the season in Los Angeles, but had a big year and won 17 games.

Then, finally, in 1956, I went to spring training and made the team — and I met Mr. Wrigley. His pattern was to go to one game in spring training and one game during the regular season — that was it. One time, as a joke, I was sent up to his office to check and see if he answered his own phone, something I didn't believe. I kept hearing these stories that Mr. Wrigley answered his own phone, rather than a secretary. Well, Mike Shawn, an executive at Arthur Meyerhoff & Company, asked me to go to the Wrigley Building and deliver a note to Mr. Wrigley — and see if he had a secretary. As it turned out, Wrigley did have a secretary, and the note asked the secretary to let me say hello to Mr. Wrigley. So, she went and told him that I was a ballplayer. He got a big smile on his face and said, "You know, you're only the third ballplayer who has ever come to see me."

When I went to Wrigley Field for the first time it was amazing — that walk up to the field from behind home plate is like no other! In one of my few starts that year I beat the Giants by a score of 7-0 and struck out Willie Mays three times. About ten years later, Jerome Holtzman wrote a story about that game because he thought it was one of the biggest achievements of my career. My record that year was 5-9, and every once in a while they would pick me to start a game, but in those years we had Bob Rush, Paul Minner, Moe Drabowsky and Dick Drott. Minner helped me a lot, Howard Pollett taught me how to throw a slider and Max Lanier helped me with my breaking ball.

In 1957, Bob Rush, the ace of the Cubs' staff, had pneumonia; Drabowsky and Drott were doing their military service for six months; and I was the number one pitcher on the team during spring training. We opened the season in St. Louis against the Cardinals and I beat them. I struck out Stan Musial twice on 3-2 curve balls in that game, which he didn't expect, because nobody had ever seen me throw a curve ball before in the Major Leagues. A week later, we were up in Chicago at Wrigley Field against the Cardinals. I was the starting pitcher and Musial was hitting fourth. I went to a count of 2-2 against him, and he just looked at a pitch that he could have hit and which I thought was a strike. The umpire called it a ball, and now we are at a 3-2 count. Then, Stan had this smile on his face. I figured he damn well knew that I was going to try and get him out with the same pitch. So, I figure, no, he will be looking for something else — anything but that curve ball. So, I threw him another 3-2 curve ball — a good one — and Musial hit it about half way up into the right field bleachers. He was laughing to himself as he rounded the bases, and when he crossed home plate he tipped his hat to me — there you go rookie! I was traded to the Cardinals in 1958, and the tenth word out of his mouth was, "Do you remember the curve ball on that 3-2 pitch?"

Jim Brosnan wrote The Longest Season, *considered one of the best baseball books ever written.*

Jim Brosnan with Cubs' Manager Bob Scheffing, 1958
Photograph by Joe Kordick *Chicago Sun-Times*

The Future: Banks, Williams and Santo | Jack Rosenberg

During the late 1950s and early '60s, it was a great time to be in Chicago. Ernie Banks, Ron Santo and Billy Williams were part of a triumvirate that was the guts of the Cubs' batting order which, year by year, just kept getting better and better. They were not only the guts of the Cubs' batting order, but they were also the guts of the Chicago sporting scene. They were the Cubs, and they were Chicago. They would spend countless hours, each season, accommodating young people with autographs. I still have a mental picture, all these years later, of those three leaning over the brick wall before a game at Wrigley Field and signing, signing, signing — and pleasing all of their fans. Then, they would go out on the field and do their thing.

Billy Williams, like Ernie Banks, was extremely quiet. At the beginning of his career, he was a disciple of the great Rogers Hornsby. From the beginning, Hornsby saw Billy's raw ability to hit, as only he could. Billy came out of Whistler, Alabama, the same general area of Alabama that spawned many great ballplayers, including Willie Mays and Willie McCovey. Billy, like Ernie, was introspective. He was one of those ballplayers who was soft-spoken, yet extremely cordial and gracious. Years later, I once went to one of the many sports banquets that we used to attend, and Billy received an award. He stood up, and after his warm, wonderful speech I thought to myself, "Can this be the same Billy Williams who I knew when he came through the minor leagues out of little Whistler, Alabama? He was and is a great man, and I have always thought highly of Billy. I was happy when he was inducted into the Hall of Fame.

Ron Santo was much more outgoing than Banks or Williams. He was outspoken and open, and really in tune with the average baseball fan — everybody knew it. He had a great demeanor about him, including a good laugh and a great personality. Glenn Beckert, the Cubs' second baseman who was Santo's roommate for many years, liked to tell a story about the time Santo was doing real well at the plate, while he was having his problems. One day Beckert went into the bathroom of the hotel room that they shared, and Santo was giving himself an injection of insulin. According to Beckert, he said to Santo, "I don't know what it is that you are taking, but give me some of it! You are hitting so well, and I'm sure that it will help me, too." You see, Santo never told his teammates he was a diabetic, and there were times when he needed to get a candy bar quickly, because he felt he might pass out on the field. He con-

trolled the disease, and in doing so Santo became a great, great hitter, a real hard-nosed ballplayer — and a phenomenal third baseman. You knew that if the ball was hit towards him, he was going to field it. I didn't get to see Brooks Robinson every day, and Brooks was as great as they came, but Santo was right with him as a defensive third baseman.

Ernie Banks came to the Chicago Cubs in September 1953 from the Kansas City Monarchs, but his first full season was in 1954, which is when I came to Chicago to work for WGN. It was also the year that Walter Alston became manager of the Brooklyn Dodgers. As the years went by, the three of us would wind up together occasionally at Wrigley Field. I would always tell them, "I've done very well, but I haven't heard too much about you two guys." They always laughed at that.

I think a lot of Ernie Banks. Ernie was tall and slender, and very quiet. It's hard to believe how he evolved from this quiet and introspective athlete to become the great spokesman for baseball and the Cubs. As a player, there wasn't any question from the beginning that he was going to be a tremendous hitter and infielder. As a hitter, when he would "wiggle" those fingers while he was holding the bat, there was nobody quite like him. We used to tell him that he "tootled the flute" — that was what it looked like. I watched him grow, and you could see his confidence grow as both a hitter and as a man — it was a thing to behold when he started to say, "Let's play two today!"

In later years, he used to go around and tell people that I had made his career, which is really unbelievable. I would say to him, "Ernie, what are you talking about?" His response was, "You got me publicized all over the country, and you were always showing tapes and videos of me — boosting me all over. You made my career." I said, "Ernie, come on, you made your career and everybody knows it."

The '50s and '60s were really something, and the heart of the Cubs' batting order is almost in the Hall of Fame. Santo isn't there yet, but he will be voted in someday soon. All three of those ballplayers, although they were just athletes, became part of the fabric of Chicago during an exciting time in the city. They went through all the joy and despair that baseball can represent. Perhaps they became bigger by losing in '69 than if they had won the pennant and World Series. Either way, it was really a great era in the history of the Cubs.

Top Left: *Ernie Banks, 1953* Top Right: *Billy Willams, 1959* Photographs by Joe Kordick

Bottom: *Ron Santo, 1960* Photograph by Bud Daley *Chicago Sun-Times*

Winning a Pennant | Billy Pierce

Before I was traded to the White Sox, I remember playing in Chicago with the Detroit Tigers in 1948. The main memory from that year was the aroma from the stockyards — it was brutal — just brutal. In fact, I figured that Chicago was one city I would never like to play in. It turns out that the aroma left — the wind blew it away, and then Comiskey Park became a beautiful place to play. The fans were always fantastic here because the team had been down for quite a few years and, as it turned out, we brought some excitement back to the city.

I was traded to the Chicago White Sox in 1948 for Aaron Robinson and $10,000 from the Detroit Tigers. I always said to Frank Lane, the Sox general manager, that maybe the $10,000 should have come to me instead, but Frank didn't seem to agree with that conclusion. You have to be lucky or you have to be good, and Frank Lane must have been both with the deals he made after he came to Chicago. I was his first trade, and while Aaron Robinson didn't stay in the league for long, I was in Chicago for many years. The next year, Lane got Nellie Fox for Joe Tipton. Tipton wasn't around for very long, and Nellie was with the White Sox for many years. In 1951, we got Minnie Minoso over here in a deal, and by the All-Star game that year we were in first place. So, it was obvious that Lane did a fantastic job for us.

The tremendous difference to me came in 1951, when we started the "Go-Go" Sox. People always think that it began in 1959, but it really began back in '51 with speedy players like Jim Rivera, Minnie Minoso and Nellie Fox. Once the "Go-Go" Sox began, the fans picked it up and began to come back to Comiskey Park. Those were big days in '51, and it marked a transition for the White Sox from a "down" team to a competitor. We had a good ball team, and we would win games with a single, stolen base, sacrifice and fly ball. By July 4, 1951, we were in first place, and we were competitive with Cleveland, Boston and New York. That was a big change.

The New York Yankees were the top team coming to town throughout the 1950s. Their pitching staff included Vic Raschi, Allie Reynolds, Tommy Byrne and Ed Lopat, and they had a great hitting team, too. Joe DiMaggio was still playing, and so was Yogi Berra, Johnny Mize, Hank Bauer, Jerry Coleman, and Phil Rizzuto. Yankee Stadium was a big thrill, and going into that ballpark, after being a kid who listened to World Series' games on radio with Mel Allen, these

were big things. I remember that the first time I went to Yankee Stadium, the visiting team locker room still had Babe Ruth's locker, before they moved it to Cooperstown. That was baseball at the highest echelon. They had a great ball club, but so did the Cleveland Indians, who were improving at that time. Cleveland always had good pitching, and they had Larry Doby, Al Rosen, Luke Easter, and Jim Hegan. However, New York had everything, including good pitching, good hitting, and great fundamentals. In the good years for the White Sox it was us, the Yankees and the Indians fighting it out for the pennant. Everyone remembers the four-game weekend series against the Yankees, including games on Friday nights and a Sunday double-header. We did that two or three times during the season and the series probably accounted for a third of our total annual attendance.

Salaries were a joke in those early years, by comparison with today. In 1945, the minimum salary was $600 a month for five and a half months, so maybe it was $3,600 a year. But, by 1949, the minimum salary was up to about $6,000 or $7,000 with a top salary of about $20,000. We only traveled by train in those days, with most games on the East Coast and no further west than St. Louis. In the 1950s, there were only eight teams each in the American and National Leagues, and the American League didn't expand to ten teams until 1961 and the National League in 1962. The trip from Boston to Chicago was a long one — I'll tell you! I remember one time we were stuck on the train — waiting and waiting. While it was stopped some farmer came by with a group of pigs. When they passed by us it just stunk. We decided that was the last straw!

When I first started out, I only had two pitches: a fast ball and a curve ball. In 1953, I finally came up with a slider, which I'd been working on for a while with Paul Richards. It took some time to get the grip right — and when I threw a good one to Hank Bauer and broke his bat I looked over in the dugout — Richards was laughing and laughing because he realized that I finally had a slider. I also threw some slow curves but I didn't have a change-up, and I never did master a good change off the fast ball. Those three pitches worked for me, and as long as I was getting by and doing fairly well, I just stayed with that combination of pitches. Before they had the Cy Young award in both leagues, I was the top pitcher in the American League in 1956 and 1957, and won 20 games during both of those years. My greatest memories of the mid-1950s were starting three All-Star games: in Cincinnati in 1953, in Milwaukee in 1955, and in Washington in 1956. I was actually on seven All-Star teams and pitched in four games, but starting an All-Star Game was the biggest thrill.

I almost had a perfect game in 1958, but Ed Fitzgerald, a catcher for the Washington Senators, got the only hit. He came in to pinch hit for Russ Kemmerer with two outs in the ninth inning. He was a first-ball/fastball hitter, so I threw him a curve ball on the outside corner. He reached out and hit it down the right field line. So, there went the perfect game. I was happy to win the ball game, and I think that as years go by I would love to have the pitch back again and try something else. I couldn't do any worse! I had four one-hitters in my career: one against New York, one against St. Louis, and two against Washington.

In 1959 — the pennant year — the only change in players that affected our team substantially was the acquisition of Ted Kluszewski from Cincinnati. Ted didn't hit that many home runs, but he hit lots of singles that knocked in some key runs for us. He became a man in our lineup who was a threat, something that we didn't have before he came to the White Sox. Bob Shaw came out of the blue as a rookie and pitched very well for us. Dick Donovan pitched well. Early Wynn had one of the best years he ever had. He came to the Sox in '58, but it was '59 when he had a real good year. Nellie Fox also had a fantastic year, and between Nellie and Luis Aparicio we had players on-base all the time. The records show that we won a lot of one-run ball games that year — that's a big thing. When you win a one-run ball game it makes you feel that you can do it again. And we did it again quite a few times.

I clearly remember the night in September 1959 when we clinched in Cleveland. Of course, they had me warming up in the bullpen in the ninth inning because Tito Francona, the left-handed hitter, was the next batter after Vic Power. But then Francona hit a ground ball to Luis Aparicio, he stepped on second, threw to first for the double play, and it was all over — the White Sox had won the pennant. We didn't know much about the sirens that were set off in Chicago that night. When we flew into the city it was about two o'clock in the morning and there was a big crowd at Midway Airport waiting to greet us. I remember after we got off the plane Earl Torgeson and I got a

cab and were going down Garfield Boulevard. People had lit flares on their lawns and were sitting outside on their steps celebrating. Everybody was out there because they were excited that the White Sox had won the pennant.

The 1959 World Series started out fantastic. Klusewski hit a couple of home runs and we won 11-0. It looked like we were going to walk away with the series against the Dodgers until the second game, when Sherm Lollar got thrown out at home plate, a play he didn't have a chance in the world of scoring on. I think that man-for-man we had a better ball club, but that doesn't mean you are going to win. It seemed that everything Larry Sherry did in the series was right. He pitched well, and if he had a ball hit hard off of him it was right at somebody. And you have to be a little lucky in this game. The Sox went on to lose the series in six games. For three days in a row, they had 92,000 people at each game in Los Angeles — some of the the biggest crowds to ever see baseball games. It was an exciting time, and to me, it was baseball at its very best.

Billy Pierce was considered one of the best left-handers in the American League during the 1950s. He finished his career with 211 victories and five All-Star Game appearances.

Billy Pierce with Ted Williams, c.1950
Billy Pierce Collection

Bill Veeck | Mary Frances Veeck

The deal for Bill to buy the White Sox from Grace Comiskey was finished at the end of the 1958 season. I still remember when we arrived in Chicago on the first day of spring in 1959 — that was quite wonderful. Bill had an enormous respect for Al Lopez, the manager of the White Sox at the time. Bill brought in a couple of players, but the team was pretty well set. Some people didn't really know what he was doing — Bill himself would always say that there was no way that we could win the pennant with this team, telling people, "You can't win with a hit batsman, a fly ball, a walk and a sacrifice bunt." But Bill was using his old psychology, and we both really believed that we had a chance with the White Sox.

Some say the "Go-Go Sox" were ready to win without Bill. Maybe so. However, his contribution, the one thing that Bill could always bring to a baseball club, was his excitement and enthusiasm. He loved baseball and he loved owning a team. He thought the idea that he could make a living in this business, something that he really did love, was wonderful. His love for the game was one of the special things that he brought to baseball — and it was contagious.

In 1959, most of the White Sox players lived at the Del Prado Hotel in Hyde Park. I think that it was one of the big differences between that era and today. I'm not saying that it was a good or bad idea, but Bill always maintained that when the teams stayed together and rode the trains together, it fostered camaraderie and a closer situation. It was very difficult to maintain a home life as a baseball player because of the constant traveling throughout the year, but I think living together in one hotel was a positive. When their husbands were on the road, the families, at least, could be together. Bill did have an absolute rule about his interaction with the players: he would never go to the same bars where the players were going to be. He was very strict about that, and thought that it was a good policy to follow. I think he was right.

The 1959 season was a great one, and I do remember the day in September when the team clinched the pennant against Cleveland. Bill was speaking downstate, and he called me and said, "'Dizzy' Trout will pick you up and drive you out to the airport, and I will meet you out there." It was so exciting, and when we got to the tarmac Mayor Daley was there with Mrs. Daley. All of a sudden, in all the commotion, I lost my shoe. So, I was kind of limping around and Mrs. Daley inquired as to the problem. I said, "I lost my shoe, I guess that I must have stepped out of it." She told the mayor the problem and he turned to somebody and said, "Find her shoe!" So, someone finally found it and held it up as if it were on a silver tray! Of course, it was just a wonderful, wonderful time. Bill and Hank Greenberg and I stayed up all night, went to a couple of places to celebrate, and sat and talked and talked.

As for the air raid sirens that were set off in celebration, we heard them but we didn't know it was going to happen. It was something that I think was done by Fire Commissioner Quinn himself. I am not even certain that Mayor Daley knew it was going to happen. I thought that when they went off it was just celebratory expression — it seemed wonderful so I wasn't panicked. After all, it was a magical night, and it seemed that the whole heavens had opened up. Later, we realized that many Chicagoans were terrified by the sirens. It was the Cold War at the time, if you recall.

In 1948, when Bill won in Cleveland, he selected the radio and television announcers for the World Series — all local personalities. Well, the networks, as well as the other club owners, were pretty upset at that decision. But Bill decided to endear himself to the local broadcasters, telecasters and newsmen. He believed strongly that because they had supported the team all those years, that they should have part of the glory. There wasn't a thing that the networks could do about it, but, needless to say, within a couple of years baseball put a rule in that the networks got to bring in their own guys to report on the World Series. Bill's lifelong policy was that you should always "go with the guys who brought you there." He felt bad about the change, and he would expound on that issue at the drop of a hat.

Bill was always thinking about the interests of the fans as well. During the World Series he limited the amount of tickets you could buy. This way whole blocks of tickets for the series wouldn't be purchased by a few buyers. Bill felt that anybody who had been a White Sox fan over the years, and supported them throughout, should have the opportunity to buy a ticket — if humanly possible. This extended to the games played in California, too — Bill gave the owner's box seats to the Comiskeys. He felt very strongly that the Comiskey family should have the owner's box, because of all those years of owning the team. Bill and I sat up in the stands and had a great time.

Mary Frances Veeck, one-time member of the Ice Capades, is the widow of the late White Sox owner, Bill Veeck.

Bill Veeck, 1959
Photograph by Luther Joseph *Chicago Sun-Times*

A World Series in Chicago

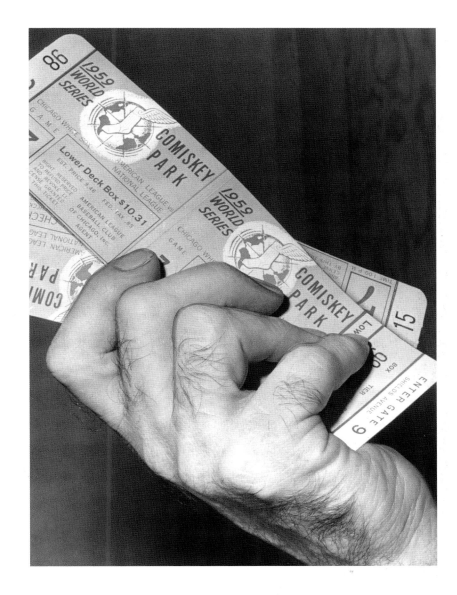

Left: *Opening Game of the World Series, October 2,1959*
Photograph by Ralph Waters *Chicago Sun-Times*

World Series Tickets, 1959
Photograph by Howard Lyon *Chicago Sun-Times*

Ted Kluszewski Celebrates 11-0 Victory in Game One, 1959
Photograph by Ralph Arvidson *Chicago Sun-Times*

Dodgers' Fans Celebrate Game Six Victory at Comiskey Park, 1959
Photograph by Ralph Arvidson *Chicago Sun-Times*

5 ENTERTAINMENT IN THE CITY

In 1950, Chicagoans had a thriving entertainment scene to enjoy, including movie theaters, ballrooms, jazz clubs, stage shows and burlesque revues, in both downtown and neighborhood locations. If residents didn't want to spend the night "on the town," they could stay at home and listen to their favorite radio broadcasts, including soap operas, serials and news programs. But a new invention began to make its way into Chicago's homes and taverns a few years earlier, one that would change the way most people had been spending their free time: television.

Over the next decade, the new medium would change the face of entertainment in the city, leaving radio behind and emptying seats in the aging theaters and clubs. In addition, a variety of other forms of entertainment would emerge in the city, too, including improvisational comedy, drive-in movies and a group of "hip" nightclubs north of the Loop. With the success of these new venues the old favorites slowly faded away — and entertainment in the city would never be the same again.

Going Out/ Staying In

Throughout the 1940s and early '50s going to the movies was still the most popular form of entertainment in the city. Since the first movie palaces were built in the 1910s and '20s, Chicagoans loved going to the "show" in these temples of cinema. The buildings brought fantastic and whimsical architecture to even the humblest of neighborhoods of the city, and with names like the Paradise, Majestic and Oriental, audiences knew they were in for something special. Even in the smaller, more modest theaters the atmosphere was charming, many with flickering stars and projected clouds on the ceiling. It was a way of life for many people, some going two or three times a week, with many kids spending all-day Saturday watching cartoons, serials and features.

Like the movie palaces, the city's ballrooms could also be lavish and grand. Even after World War II, a time when the ballrooms thrived, couples still liked to go for dinner and dancing at the Aragon, Trianon, Milford and Edgewater Beach Hotel ballrooms, all offering live music in settings that were romantic and glamorous. Many smaller "dine and dance" clubs were also located throughout the city, but offered entertainment on a more limited scale. Venues like Olsen's Theater Restaurant on North Avenue and the 5100 Club on Broadway were less expensive then the big clubs, but were still popular with patrons.

By 1950, television was gaining in popularity. The transition began innocently enough as local stations like WENR, WGN and WBKB began to broadcast sporting events, included boxing, wrestling and baseball. Most viewers had to watch these broadcasts in their neighborhood taverns, where many of the first sets appeared. Early televisions could cost as much as $1000.00, so the introduction into the mainstream market was slow. Chicagoans were curious about the invention, however, and learned more about the new medium wherever they could, like a friend's or neighbor's home, or by lingering in front of an appliance store window.

In the meantime, many Chicagoans remained faithful to their favorite radio programs, despite the growing interest in television. Don McNeil's "Breakfast Club," "Ma Perkins" and "Lux Radio Theater" were all local favorites, but as many of the big radio stars left for new careers in television, radio listeners had little choice but to follow their favorites to the "small" screen. At first, many radio performers would do both television and radio broadcasts, skeptical about the future of television, particularly since the medium had been around for years without breakout success. Eventually, with the great television success of former radio stars like Jack Benny and Burns and Allen, it would be impossible to stop the creative losses felt in radio.

Chicago Television

In the early days of television, programming was still irregular. While the city had four major stations, WBKB - Channel 4, WNBQ - Channel 5, WENR - Channel 7 and WGN - Channel 9, they were still in the early stages of developing content. Sports programming, inexpensive and easy to produce, filled many hours of the day, including baseball, football, boxing and lots of wrestling. While this programming was popular, it wasn't until a wider variety of programming was available that viewership really took off.

Of course, critical to television viewership was television ownership, and that's where Polk Bros played an important role. Polk Bros began in 1935 when Sol Polk and his five siblings opened a small appliance store on the Northwest Side. By the early 1950s, they grew to three locations, with nearly 8000 shoppers a day buying refrigerators, stoves and televisions — lots of televisions. Their huge success was due in part to their early leadership in television advertising, which began in 1949 when they bought time on WBKB. Some questioned their strategy of advertising television sets on television — logic dictated most people watching already owned sets — or so it seemed. But Sol Polk knew that there were just as many people viewing early television who didn't own a set yet, instead watching wherever they could. Polk Bros quickly became one of the biggest advertisers in town by sponsoring over 25 hours of programming a week, including favorites like "Lunchtime Little Theater," "Polk's Playhouse" and "Kup's Show." The strategy would prove to be hugely successful.

Those that did own sets in the early days of television were treated to some lively and innovative shows originating from the city, including those produced by the "Chicago School of Television," a label given programs produced here that were both entertaining and thoughtful. Good examples of the Chicago School include "Stud's Place,"created by and starring Studs Terkel, which first aired in 1949 as part of a variety show called "Saturday Night Square." The largely improvised show got its own time slot in 1950 and ran until 1951, when it lost sponsorship. Dave Garroway's "Garroway at Large" was a loose, low-key show that began in Chicago in 1949. He moved the show to New York City and eventually became the first host of the "Today" show on NBC. "Junior Jamboree," a show that featured the puppet mastery of Burr Tillstrom, debuted on WBKB in 1947. In 1949, the show moved to NBC and was renamed "Kukla, Fran and Ollie," airing five days a week at 6:00 pm. Many others got their start in Chicago before moving to bigger network jobs, including Mike Wallace, Hugh Downs, Marlin Perkins and Mike Douglas.

Children's programming was popular from the start in Chicago. The first shows could be somewhat primitive, with simple sets and production values, but they did have a charming "let's put on a show" quality. Beginning in 1952, Dr. Frances Horwich, known to Chicago kids as "Miss Frances," hosted "Ding Dong School" on WNBQ. Her schoolmarmish charm endeared her to children as they learned simple lessons in reading and math. Also in 1952, Frazier Thomas' "Garfield Goose & Friends" debuted on WBKB at 4:30 in the afternoon, opposite the "Howdy Doody Show." The program's "magic drawing board" and "Little Theater" segments were favorites that kept the show running into the 1980s. In 1953, "Noontime Comics" with Uncle Johnny Coons debuted, and was a big hit with the city's elementary school children watching during their lunch break from school. The structure of the show was simple, with Uncle Johnny eating his lunch while showing cartoons and teaching lessons in right and wrong. Also that year Ray Rayner could first be seen on "The Ray Rayner Show," a teenage dance program that ran from 1953 to 1958 on WBBM. However, it was the WGN children's show of the same name that had the bigger impact.

As kids got older and grew out of children's programming, Chicago television had many shows that appealed to teenagers. "Bandstand Matinee," hosted by Jim Lounsbury, was similar to Dick Clark's "American Bandstand," but with a local flavor. The WGN show featured mostly Chicago area performers, including local high school, YMCA and park district acts. Beginning in 1963, "Kiddie a Go-Go," began on WLS, and featured many top name musical groups that came through Chicago. As rock and roll music became more popular with teens, so did these shows.

Adults tended to be more interested in the national programming broadcast during the prime time hours. It was the golden age of television during the 1950s and everyone had their favorites, including "The Honeymooners," "Lawrence Welk," "Ed Sullivan," "Playhouse 90," "Philco Theater," "Kraft Television Playhouse," "Gunsmoke," "Bonanza," "I Love Lucy," "Wanted-Dead or Alive," "The Rifleman," "Our Miss Brooks," "I Remember Mama" or one of the many game or quiz show broadcasts. Local newscasts were also popular, and viewers had many great television journalists to chose from, including Ulmer Turner on WBKB-Channel 4, Austin Kiplinger on WENR-Channel 7, Fahey Flynn and P.J. Hoff on WBBM-Channel 2, and

Len O'Connor, Clifton Utley and Jim Hurlbut on WNBQ-Channel 5. Sporting events and B-movies dominated the rest of programming, and with the addition of public television station WTTW in 1955, viewers had a wide variety of shows to choose from.

Sad Endings, New Beginnings

As television began to dominate the attention of more and more Chicagoans, the city's most popular entertainment venues saw their audience numbers dwindle. Long-standing favorite outings, like seeing feature films in the big movie palaces, became less of an attraction, leaving the enormous venues with many empty seats. The Loop was hardest hit, and by the mid-1960s, a time of tremendous social change and upheaval, many residents were left feeling uncomfortable or afraid to go downtown at night, severely affecting traffic at theaters, clubs and restaurants.

It was almost unimaginable. For years, Chicagoans loved to go downtown, seeing Merriel Abbott productions at the Conrad Hilton and the big stage shows at the Shubert or Palace. But tastes were changing, and fewer people were interested in these shows or the aging venues they were held. The big Loop palaces, as well as the large capacity neighborhood theaters like the Norshore and the Marbro, would suffer the most. In 1957, the Norshore was razed. In 1963, the Marbro came down, as well as Adler and Sullivan's historic Garrick Theater in the Loop — and it was just the beginning.

While the changing tastes left some of the city's most beloved institutions shuttered, new forms of entertainment were beginning to emerge around Chicago — on a much different scale. North of the Loop, on stages smaller and more intimate than the big downtown venues, innovative new acts were gaining popularity with younger audiences. Folk singers, like the New Lost City Ramblers and Pete Seeger, began appearing at the Gate of Horn and the Fickle Pickle. Bright, edgy comedians like Lenny Bruce and Jackie Mason began appearing at clubs like Mister Kelly's and Tradewinds. "Coffee house" performances, including poetry readings and pantomimists, could be found in small storefront theaters like the Blind Pig and the Happy Medium.

Perhaps most successful was the style of improvisational theater pioneered in Chicago by the Compass Players in 1956, led by director Paul Sills and a company including Mike Nichols, Elaine May and Shelley Berman. The group first appeared in the back room of Jimmy's Tavern on 55th Street, then at the Dock in Lake Park, before relocating to St. Louis in 1957. In 1959, Second City opened in a former Chinese laundry on Wells Street and continued the format created by the Compass Players. The influence of these two groups on American comedy is immeasurable, with many great comedians like Barbara Harris, Alan Arkin and Joan Rivers getting started there in the early days.

Then, in 1960, Hugh Hefner, already a leader in publishing, opened the Playboy Club on the Near North Side. Through his club, magazine and WBKB television show, "Playboy's Penthouse," Hefner realized an entirely new vision of night life, one that was very different from the Loop's aging hotel and bar scene. His world appealed to the younger generation of Chicagoans who had their own interests in music, art and politics — sharply contrasting with those of their parents.

The success of the Playboy Club and other new venues contributed to an entertainment vacuum that left the old favorites struggling for life. But it was television, more then any other form of entertainment, that changed the way Chicagoans spent their free time — and still dominates today.

Page 188: *Harvest Moon Dance at Chicago Stadium, 1950*
Photograph by Ralph Walters *Chicago Sun-Times*

In Performance

Tony Bennett at Fenger High School, 1956
Photograph by Larry Nocerino *Chicago Sun-Times*

Duke Ellington at Ravinia Park, 1957
Photograph by Bill Knefel *Chicago Sun-Times*

Dean Martin and Jerry Lewis at Chicago Stadium, c.1950

Irv Kupcinent, Peggy Lee, Bob Hope and
Frank Sinatra at Civic Opera House, 1950
Photograph by Joe Kordick *Chicago Sun-Times*

Jane Russell at Lions Club Convention, 1958
Photograph by Bill Pauer *Chicago Sun-Times*

Dancers at the Latin Quarter, c.1956

Dinah Shore Performs at Dinner for President Eisenhower, 1958
Photograph by Bill Pauer *Chicago Sun-Times*

Jack Benny at Civic Opera House, 1958
Photograph by Bill Knefel *Chicago Sun-Times*

A Life in Music Begins | Ramsey Lewis

I was 15 years old and still at Wells High School in 1950. I had just joined the musicians' union by telling them I was 16. They didn't ask for any proof, so I started playing with a band called the Cleffs. Wallace Burton was the leader of the Cleffs, and after he heard me playing the piano in church he invited me to come over to his house. Wallace told me what jazz records to buy and listen to — he was really the one who whetted my appetite in terms of jazz. If it had not been for him, we wouldn't be talking about jazz today — he was the one who got me started.

When you are 15 years old, playing in a musical group was just something to do on weekends. And if you picked up $5 or $6, in those days, it wasn't loose change. I pretended to play jazz piano, but I think in my heart I was still going to be a classical musician.

The Korean War broke up our seven-piece group, and Eldee Young and I were the only two guys who didn't go. In those days, if you were in college, you were deferred from military service until they needed you. During those years, we were pretty much part of the wallpaper at a nightclub called the Lake Meadows Lounge, on 35th and South Parkway. We played music, but people weren't as attentive as we wanted them to be. A few people came in just to hear us, and one of them was Daddy-O Daylie, a big-time disc jockey on WAIT-AM in those days. He would come in there to hear us, and one of the times he said, "You know, you guys are pretty good. You should have a record deal." We had heard that before, but he came back a couple of weeks later and said, "I've arranged an audition for you with a record company. On Saturday, show up at 48th and Cottage Grove at a stationary store that is owned by the Chess brothers — they are just starting a label."

So, we showed up at their place on Saturday. They had a piano in the shipping department and we set up and played three or four songs. Phil Chess was smoking his pipe and said, "Yeah, you guys are pretty good." So, Phil called Sonny to the shipping department and asked him, "What do you think of these guys?" We played a couple more times and Sonny said, "These guys are really good." So, Phil told us that he wanted to talk to his brother, Leonard, and he would get back to us. About a week later, Daddy-O called and told us that they wanted to sign our trio — we got our first record deal.

In the early days, the Chess family had already recorded the blues and they knew the best blues makers around — they ended up with some of the best blues artists ever. They kind of left what to play up to us, because they didn't know quite what to do. Phil Chess used to say, "Play more high notes, play more high notes!" I didn't know what that meant! We were pretty much left up to our own devices, and we recorded an album called "The Gentlemen of Swing." The album sat on the shelf for awhile, and they were not certain if they wanted to put it out. Daddy-O Daylie said to them, "If you put it out in Chicago, I guarantee that I will play it." So, they did put it out in Chicago, he played it, and then Marty Faye and others played it, and we became fairly well-known because of their support.

We played the London House in Chicago for eight to ten weeks a year, every year, for many years. In those days, you went into the studio every six months and did another album. For us, every new album became a little more popular, and we were pretty happy with that. But it wasn't until we recorded our 17th album that we had our first big hit. A couple of months after the album was out, we got a call from the record company saying that we had a big hit on our hands. We didn't quite understand what that meant, because we didn't record albums in those days to be "big hits." We recorded them because that's the way we felt about music at that time. So, we asked, "What song are they playing?" They told us it was the song called "The In-Crowd." We found that to be very humorous because "The In-Crowd" was the final song we put on the album. After that, there were several other hits and we got booked all over the United States in the major concert halls and nightclubs.

Chicago was a special place to develop my musical talent, and it remains special because it has such a diversification in music — various cultures and ethnic groups that you are exposed to. In Chicago, unlike New York City, a jazz musician could allow himself to be influenced by blues, R&B, gospel, and classical music. In New York, you had to tow the line in terms of Charlie Parker and Bud Powell. That was some of the greatest music that was ever played, but blues, R&B and gospel were sort of pushed aside. In Chicago, you could do whatever you wanted. If you wanted to play blues or gospel or your own version of a Beethoven sonata — whatever — do it man! During my most impressionable years, from the age of eight to sixteen years, that's the music I heard all day, every day, seven days a week — classical music, gospel music, and, eventually, jazz. There it is!

Ramsey Lewis has recorded over 70 albums during his career. His radio show can be heard weekday mornings on WNUA.

London House, Michigan and Wacker, 1959

Rock and Roll For Sale | Ed Yalowitz

My interest in music started in the late 1940s when I began taking piano lessons downtown. Once a week I took the Illinois Central train from South Shore to Van Buren Street and then walked over to the Fine Arts Building at 412 S. Michigan Avenue. Near there, at Adams and Wabash, was Hudson Ross, one of the largest record stores in Chicago at that time. They had listening booths where, before purchasing the records, you could audition music recorded by popular artists of the day, like Patti Page, Nat King Cole and Frankie Laine.

After college I worked for a short time for a local Chicago FM radio station, and then got the opportunity to work in the music business — a dream come true. My uncle was appointed the Chicago and surrounding area distributor for ABC Paramount, a division of ABC Broadcasting Company. The company released their first record in 1955 which was the very popular theme song from "The Mickey Mouse Show." It was an immediate best seller, and we joined a small but growing group of independent record distributors in the city. Prior to that time the major labels, including RCA, Columbia, Decca, London and Capitol, dominated the music scene and controlled most of the market.

In those days, our customers were mainly independent record dealers like Hudson Ross, Rose Records and Polk Bros. In addition, there were literally hundreds of small storefront independent record retailers throughout the city and suburbs. It is also important to note that records were sold and promoted through jukebox operators, who placed their machines in locations throughout the city. This was a very effective way to introduce a newly released record to the public.

By the mid-1950's the music business began to change dramatically. Vinyl 45's and long playing albums ("LPs") that were light in weight and almost non-breakable replaced the heavy, fragile 78-RPM records made from shellac. More importantly, at the same time, kids discovered Bill Haley and The Comets when they recorded and released "Rock Around The Clock." The record hit like a bombshell and was probably the first rock and roll record to achieve national popularity — the rock and roll era was born. Suddenly there was a major shift in the musical tastes of teenagers as they thirsted for more and more rock and roll music. Small labels sprung up overnight releasing rock artists and selling their records through the network of independent distributors all over the country. Among the early stars was Carl Perkins, the first to record "Blue Suede Shoes." After Perkins, RCA Victor, a major record label, realized the potential of rock

and signed Elvis Presley, who was discovered by Sam Phillips, owner of Sun Records in Memphis. At first, disc jockeys at the pop radio stations hesitated to play this "wild music," but teenagers' demand for his records was so overwhelming that they had to play his records, whether they liked him or not. Of course, Elvis' appearance on "The Ed Sullivan Show" enhanced his national popularity, too. With that, the barrier was broken and pop radio stations throughout the country began to feature rock and roll — and a new era in music began.

Our company began to add independent record companies to the roster, as did other distributors. Then, in the late 1950's, another change in musical tastes began to take place, arguably the most important of all — the crossover of rhythm & blues into the popular market. Artists like Ray Charles, Lloyd Price, Muddy Waters, Wilson Pickett and Otis Redding, who had previously sold records mainly to the black community, were now becoming popular with teens across the country.

I was right in the middle of this evolution, and worked with many of the recording artists as well as the radio personalities who played their records. WIND's Howard Miller, Chicago's most popular disc jockey in the '50s, had the listening audience to create the demand for a record overnight once he began to play it. Of course there were others at WIND who were influential, including Dick Williamson, Milo Hamilton, Bernie Allen, and program director Fred Saliano. Other popular broadcasters in Chicago at that time included Dick Biondi, Clark Weber, Art Roberts, Eddie Hubbard and Jim Lounsbury, who hosted the popular Chicago teenage dance show, "Bandstand Matinee," fashioned after Dick Clark's national dance show, "American Bandstand." When a recording artist came to Chicago, we would introduce them to the disc jockeys, who would then play their latest records and perhaps interview them on the air. We also would make appearances with the recording artists at record stores and sock hops. We handled the recordings of many of the best selling singers of that era, like Ray Charles, Paul Anka, Frankie Avalon, Edie Gorme and Danny and the Juniors, just to name a few.

Of course, there was another monumental change in popular music in 1964, when the Beatles revolutionized the record business — again.

Ed Yalowitz attended South Shore High School and the University of Illinois before his career in the record business.

Sock Hop Hosted by WIND Disc Jockey Howard Miller, 1956

Souvenir Photo, Sir?

Almost every fancy Chicago restaurant and nightclub offered souvenir photos in the 1950s. The process was simple — a photographer would approach a table of patrons and offer to take a picture. If accepted, the photo would be ready by the end of dinner, placed in a colorful folder with the name and logo of the venue. There was a catch, however, because if the photo wasn't washed in water later by the customer it would gradually get darker and darker, eventually turning black.

Bismark Hotel's Swiss Chalet, 1952

Rhumboogie Nightclub, c.1950

Old Heidelburg, 1950

Olsen's Theatre Restaurant, c.1950

Jimmy Durante Joins Patrons at Chez Paree, c.1950

Joe '40,000' Murphy

Andy Frain usher Joe "40,000" Murphy worked for nearly 50 years in Chicago's ballparks, stadiums and convention halls. During these events, Murphy would have his picture taken with celebrities, politicians and local dignitaries, which he would then use to cover the walls of his Bridgeport home and garage. These photos of Jimmy Durante and Jayne Mansfield are just two of thousands Murphy collected during his lifetime.   Bill Swislow Collection

A Short History of Television in Chicago | Steve Jajkowski

The history of television in Chicago goes back to the 1920s, when there were many experiments in television, including WCFL. They operated a radio station, but they also started experimenting with television transmissions. On June 19, 1928 they performed a major experiment when they filmed the head of one of their secretaries, E.N. Nichols. The video portion was transmitted on short-wave frequencies on W9XAA, while the audio was transmitted on WCFL radio. Short-wave was not a very reliable frequency spectrum to work for television, however, because there was too much sun spot and atmospheric interference to really make it work.

In the 1930s, there were three or four television stations using a mechanical broadcast system, but still nothing like we have today. The *Chicago Daily News* began a broadcasting station on August 27, 1930, which lasted until August 31, 1933. It combined audio on WMAQ-AM over a 100-watt transmitter from 400 W. Madison, with a video broadcast on W9XAP. The station had regular programming schedules in the daily newspapers, although they were only on a couple of hours each day. The shows might include a magician doing little tricks or a vaudeville act, with the emphasis on action rather than dialogue. The technology wasn't very good at the time, with the big problem being the size of the screen — it wasn't much bigger than a small hamburger — only a couple of inches wide, and the resolution wasn't very clear either. Televisions that we have today are usually 441 lines per resolution, while the high definition TVs are 1,000 lines per resolution. These old mechanical sets were only 30 lines per resolution, so there was no way that it was going to sell.

In 1939, the first electronic station to broadcast began on W9XZV, a station owned by the Zenith Radio Corporation. At the time, Zenith was only manufacturing radios and phonograph players, but wanted to get into broadcasting, so they got a construction permit to operate on Channel 1. Eugene McDonald, the chairman of Zenith at the time, had a vision of television that was quite different than everybody else. His idea was that television should not be commercialized, but should be pay-per-view. This way, viewers would pay through subscription, and programming would not be saturated with advertising. The station was very low power, and they probably only had a transmission range of 30 miles on a windy day. Two of the early Chicago television personalities on Channel 1 were Pat Buttram, who was later on television as the sidekick for Gene Autrey, and Tommy Bartlett, who would have the water show in the

Wisconsin Dells. However, there were not a lot of people who had television sets to watch these programs.

When war broke out in 1941, the FCC said that no stations could broadcast except for those that could prove they could be on the air for a reliable amount of time each day. In Chicago, only WBKB, headed by John Balaban of Paramount's Balaban and Katz movie theater chain, could meet the requirements. The station was one of only a handful in the country that was allowed to broadcast during the war years.

After 1946, more attention was beginning to be paid to television, but there still wasn't much regular programming yet. Most programming was local, and the networks hadn't really kicked in. It wasn't until 1948 that there was major network programming — Milton Berle and the Texaco Star Theater went on the air in that year. By 1949, programming could be found regularly on a number of stations in Chicago, including WBKB on Channel 4, WENR on Channel 7, WGN on Channel 9 and WNBQ on Channel 5, but most stations focused heavily on sports. Remember, during the late 1940s most of the televisions in Chicago were in taverns, and sports appealed to those audiences. Sports programming was on all the channels, including boxing and wrestling — it was cheap programming for the stations. In fact, for several years, Cubs games were broadcast on two channels — 4 and 9. Not surprisingly, Channel 9 was big on sports right from the beginning, including home games of both the Cubs and the White Sox, wrestling, boxing and Northwestern University football.

About that time, Sterling "Red" Quinlan, the General Manager of WBKB, began thinking about different ways to make television more cosmopolitan. He sought to broaden its appeal, particularly for housewives and children, so that televisions could be put into homes, as well as bars. Red worried that if television remained focused on sports entirely, it would take a lot longer before people's homes would have been the place to watch TV. Red was an innovator — he hired Lee Phillip for WBKB, and he had another morning show with Bob Murphy and Kay Westphall, which was a loosely formatted "coffee klatch" kind of morning talk show. It was the development of these shows that pushed sales of televisions, and soon they were appearing in living rooms across Chicagoland.

Steve Jajkowski is a television historian who writes extensively about the development of the medium in Chicago.

'Have a Coke on Polk' | Bruce Bachmann

My mother's family emigrated to America from Romania in 1906, when she was only three years old. Her name, Ghisela Pokovitz, became Goldie Polk after the family name was Americanized. Soon after, the family grew in size, as parents Henry and Yetta Pokovitz, welcomed five more children, all boys: Sam, Harry, Morris, David and Sol.

The family's first store was called Central Avenue Appliance and Furniture until 1947, when the name was changed to Polk Bros (yes, without the period!). My mother and her brothers ran the business, but my Uncle Sol, the youngest of the family, was the "mover and shaker." After he went into the service during World War II he continued to run things through the use of V-mails. In reality, however, there was nothing to sell because there weren't any new appliances being made, and even immediately after the war people still didn't have a lot of money to spend. It wasn't until the servicemen returned and started earning some real money that things turned around. Once they bought houses they needed appliances — lots of appliances. In those days, new homes didn't come with refrigerators or stoves so people had to buy their own appliances — and Polk Bros didn't have much competition.

Sol started the discount approach from day one, and there was a void in the market because the other appliance dealers in town, including Goldblatts and Marshall Field's, didn't discount. In fact, there were no other discounters, so Polk Bros just blossomed with low overhead and not very good looking stores. You can't go into a good looking store and get a good deal! If the carpet was old and frayed it meant they were passing the savings on to the customer — and that mystique worked. The greatest growth for Polk Bros was from 1949 to 1955.

I was very lucky because I lived above the Polk Bros store on Central and Diversey. We always had a television set, but nearly everyday we had to get a new one because they would sell the television set we were watching. Televisions were pretty rare in those days, so neighbors would come to our house because we were one of the few families with a set. Even after we moved back to the Austin neighborhood, sure enough, a Polk Bros truck would pull in front of our apartment, maybe once a week, dragging our television set out because they had sold it.

Polk Bros became an icon during the 1950s because of the circus atmosphere there, including clowns in the store and giveaways such as Georgia watermelons and California oranges. There was always a Polk on the floor at the stores, and my Uncle Harry often posed sitting on top of a stove with a pencil and pad in his hands, giving people "a deal!" Of course, you got a better deal by not talking to a Polk, but no one knew that. In those days, people wanted special deals, so everybody claimed to know Sol Polk, or went to school with him, or claimed to be his cousin.

Part of Polk Bros success at the time was due to their heavy advertising in the early days of television. They ran their first ad on WBKB in 1949, which was before most people even had televisions. Soon after, they were averaging about 25 hours a week of television sports. They were one of the biggest advertisers in Chicago, sponsoring shows like "Polk's Playhouse" and "Kup's Show." They were real innovators.

Polk Bros was also the first company to give in-house credit. Keep in mind, there was no Visa or Mastercard in those days. Credit sales became a huge revenue source for the company because they didn't need to make a profit on the appliances — not if they were making 12% on the credit purchases!

Another Polk Bros innovation in those years was trade-ins. Now, most people think you are doing the customer a favor by taking the old refrigerator as a trade-in, but we made the most of them. In fact, we ran it like the used car business — we were selling shiploads of old appliances to South America and Mexico. In fact, we had a store that sold nothing but used appliances that we reconditioned — and made money there, too.

Over the years, Polk Bros rode a tide of success until the big box stores took over the volume purchasing/selling idea. Polk Bros stores weren't the first on everyone's minds anymore, so we began to scale down. The worst moment came when I had the task of telling my mother that our store at North and First Avenues had burned. In addition to being our most productive location, it also housed our offices and distribution center. All of the Polk Brothers were gone, and now a tragic fire had destroyed the main store.

But the legacy of the Polk Bros lives on through our foundation, and giving back to the city seems only right, since Chicago is our home.

Bruce Bachmann is a real estate and development financier who serves as a board member of the Polk Bros Foundation.

What's on Television?

"Miss Tavern Pale Beauty Contest" on WGN, 1950
Mayor Daley Addresses Chicago on WTTW, c.1958

Mike Douglas' "Hi Ladies" on WGN, 1956

Lee Phillip's "Meet Miss Lee" on WBBM, c.1956
Lee Phillip Bell Collection

Mary Hartline's "Princess Mary's Magic Castle" on WBKB, c.1957
Museum of Broadcast Communications Chicago

TV Journalist and Commentator Clifton Utley on WNBQ, 1955

TV Weatherman Clint Youle on WNBQ, 1957

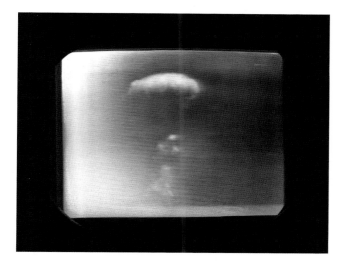

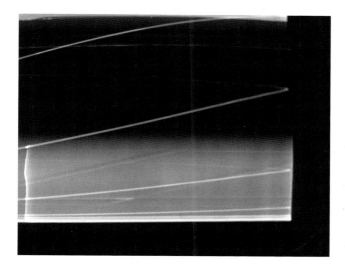

Chicago Broadcast of Atomic Bomb Test on WNBQ, 1952

Missing Radio/ Loving Television | Chuck Schaden

I was an avid listener of radio in the late 1940s, even though television was quickly gaining in popularity. I still loved to listen to the radio, just as I did in the earlier part of the decade. But we were challenged by television, and since everyone else was excited about television coming on the scene, we could hardly wait to get a set in our own home to see what all of our radio favorites looked like. As it turned out we were disappointed, because they didn't look the way that we had thought they looked. In a few cases there were people whom we had already seen, like Bob Hope, who had been in the movies. However, other radio stars from shows like "Our Miss Brooks," "My Friend Irma" and "Life with Luigi" didn't look exactly like we had pictured them. I think each listener had a different idea of what the radio stars looked like, so there would always be a little disappointment there.

When television came on the scene it was an amazing thing. Everyone was waiting for it. The only television most kids had seen was from the outside looking in, like through a tavern window. There was a man across the street from us who had the first television set in the neighborhood. It was probably in 1948, because we had our first television in 1949. This man built a little theater in his basement with seats, and he would let the neighbors come in freely to watch television on his tiny 10-inch screen. We would go there after supper and watch, and there would be as many as 14 people in his basement.

There was a second guy on the block who had a television set, and we would also go to his house. Until we got our own television set, we were the biggest freeloaders you could ever find! When we went to his house, we would bring popcorn or food to help pay our way. Then, finally, we got a television set. My father was sold on the Zenith round screen television because he felt that we got a bigger picture with the round screen. It was a 10-inch screen in a large console, and I can't imagine what he paid for it. Indeed, we did get a bigger picture with the round screen, but what we didn't realize was that all pictures being broadcast at that time were rectangular pictures, so while you enlarged the picture it actually cut the corners off.

Every program was my "favorite" program in those years. Of course, in the early days you watched anything that was on television. We sat with a tray and a TV dinner for 15 minutes watching the test pattern before the stations even signed on in the evening. The way that television operated in the very early days was that the stations were on and off intermittently. They would broadcast for two hours in the afternoon and then sign off, then come back at 6:00 p.m. Channel 9 might carry a Cubs game that would be over around 4:00 p.m., then they might have an hours worth of programming, and then the station would sign off. They just didn't have any regular programming in the early days of television because there weren't enough viewers.

Sometime in the 1950s, I remember there was a service called Phone-a-Vision, an early form of "cable" television. They transmitted a scrambled picture, but you could still hear audio. If you were hooked up to the service, you could call them up and they would unscramble the picture, then you could watch a movie. I remember one day they had a movie on at 2:00 in the afternoon, and then repeated it at 6:00 and 8:00 at night. We didn't subscribe to the service, but we would "watch" the movie with the scrambled picture and listen to the sound. I sat there six hours that day watching scrambled pictures and listening to the movie, and I had a terrible headache that I couldn't get rid of for three days!

As the years progressed I watched everything I could on television. On Monday nights it was "Godfrey's Talent Scouts" and "I Love Lucy." Tuesday nights we would watch Uncle Miltie. Wednesday nights it was "The Kraft Television Theater" and "Arthur Godfrey and Friends" — we watched everything! For me, personally, I thought that it was nice, but I also remembered radio so well. I would turn on the radio and nothing was there anymore. Almost all the radio programs that I used to listen to were gone, except for maybe "Suspense" on Sunday afternoons, and only a very few other programs. So, I was really disappointed that all the old radio shows were gone, and radio had changed to just disc jockeys playing music. Radio hung in there pretty well until the mid-1950s, and there were a few things on CBS that stayed until around 1962.

After I graduated from high school, I went to college at the University of Illinois at Navy Pier for two years. While I was there I discovered that there was a radio station in Elmwood Park, and I went over there one day to see what it was doing. It was a little FM station called WLEY, for Leyden Township, located on Harlem, just about two blocks north of Grand Avenue. During 1953 and 1954 I got the chance to do some work on the station — my first real broadcasting experience — and the beginning of my own career in radio.

Chuck Schaden, member of the Chicago Journalism Hall of Fame, is best known for his popular radio program "Those Were the Days."

Milton Berle Visits WIND Studios, c.1950

'Here is Something Just Handed Me!' | Hugh Downs

My network broadcast career started in Chicago in 1943 at NBC's Central Division. I still had a terrible case of "mike fright" at the time, and I don't know why it took me such a long time to get over it. One of my first programs was called "The Voice of Firestone," where I substituted for the regular announcer. It was a classical music program, and, although I was happy to do it, I was terrified. I had to hold a script in one hand while grabbing my lapel and pulling down so that it wouldn't shake and the paper wouldn't rattle. I was really fortunate in that even though my knees turned to jelly and my blood turned to ice water, it never showed in my voice — and nobody could ever tell that I was scared to death.

It was an interesting time to be in Chicago because many of the network shows originated from there. The bulk of the daytime soap operas came from Chicago, and, as a matter of fact, I was an announcer on a few of them. Once I even got an acting job on one when an actor failed to show up! I used to do standby announcing for "Ma Perkins," one of the most popular soap operas of the day, but I was also the regular announcer for "John's Other Wife" and a hospital-based soap opera called "Back Stage Wife," starring Ken Griffin. I also did 5-10 minute news broadcasts during those years for the network, mainly on Sunday mornings for over 80 stations. The major news broadcasts were done in the evening by people like H.V. Kaltenborn, and I wasn't doing those yet because I didn't have that kind of visibility or experience in those days.

I remember when John Chancellor, who was Jack Chancellor then, was a writer in the NBC newsroom in Chicago. He used to prepare things for my broadcasts in those days. Now, Chancellor was a great prankster, and one Sunday morning I had come to work in a dense fog and I had parked in front of the Merchandise Mart. I went up to the studio and the first thing I had to do was this newscast, and Chancellor, with a straight face, brought in the newscast copy. I started to read it, and about a minute into it he came in with another piece of paper and handed it to me — this happened often, like some breaking news — and I said, "Here is something just handed me!" Well, it said that the owner of a 1948 Packard parked in front of the Merchandise Mart is going to be very embarrassed when he finds his battery dead — that was my car! Chancellor was an interesting guy. He drove a convertible, and he always insisted that a convertible is an automobile with a cloth top that you only put up when it rains. He always left the top down, even in subzero weather! Of course, he went on to become the host of the NBC prime time newscast in New York.

Things began to change for me at NBC when television came in. In 1945, I did my first television program, but it wasn't with NBC, because they were not on television in Chicago until about 1949. Instead, I did a program at WBKB, which was the Balaban and Katz experimental station in the B&K theater. It was regular electronic scanning beam television, the kind that would become television as we know it. It was kind of amusing to me because not only did I not own a television set yet, but had never seen a television program! My first broadcast was really just a televised radio newscast, because they didn't have any film footage or anything like that. It was just 15 minutes of a camera on me reading the news. So, after I did the program I told them that I had never seen a television program before — even though I had just been on a television program! The producer said, "Well, we are going to do another show in 45 minutes, and there is a set in the lobby, so you can watch that program." So, I went out and bought a sandwich, and came back to the lobby and sat there and watched my first television program — after I had broadcast my first one. The story is a little weird, but it's true.

It wasn't until around 1950 that I did any serious television. I was the announcer for "Kukla, Fran and Ollie," and, once in a while I would appear on screen with Fran Allison and the puppet characters. It really took me a while to realize that "the tail was going to wag the dog of broadcasting" — then I got heavily into television. I was in Chicago until April of 1954, when I moved to New York City. Dave Garroway had already left Chicago in '52 to start "The Today Show" there. When I left in '54, I was an occasional guest with Dave on "Today" and didn't know, at that time, that I was going to be doing that show for ten years, replacing Garroway. In the beginning, I really didn't know whether I would be coming back to Chicago or not, but I finally took root in New York, and television was very kind to me.

Hugh Downs, one of the best known television personalities of the twentieth century, began a radio career in Michigan before coming to Chicago in the 1940s.

Hugh Downs at Home in Wilmette, Illinois, c.1950
University of Wyoming Archives

Getting Started in Chicago | Mike Wallace

I graduated from the University of Michigan in 1939 and then worked in Grand Rapids and Detroit radio for a couple of years. I announced radio programs at those stations, as well as all manner of chores that included newscasts and some "color" commentary for sports events. I got to Chicago in 1941, and I was there until 1943, when I left for service in the Navy.

From 1941 to 1943, I'd mainly done freelance radio work in Chicago as well as regular broadcasts of the radio edition of the *Chicago Sun*, a late night newscast on WMAQ. I worked out of the Merchandise Mart and can recall that Hugh Downs and Dave Garroway, who also spent their early broadcasting years in Chicago, would sit in the WMAQ announcers' lounge with a huge Webster's dictionary — the kind that was placed on wheels. For a buck a word, they'd try to stump each other with words that they may or may not have known. I remember their contest involved rolling that dictionary back and forth between them — it was quite a sight.

I returned to Chicago from the Navy in 1946. I was primarily doing radio, though television was just beginning at that time. A fellow by the name of Don Elder had replaced me at WMAQ, but they had to give me my job back since that was the law for people who came back to their jobs from WWII. I had a variety of jobs during those years, including news, and at WJWC, owned by Marshall Field, I worked for Clifton Utley. It was during those postwar years that I changed my name from Myron Wallace to Mike Wallace because NBC wanted to do a program called "For The Love of Mike," a kind of afternoon variety hour where I would interview people and play music. I also announced radio soap operas, the news on WBBM, and the "Sky King" radio show. In addition, when I first came back from the Navy, I did a show called "Famous Names" on WGN radio that was broadcast live out of the Balinese Room of the Blackstone Hotel. It was an interview show with people who were in town to perform at Chicago theaters and vaudeville houses. So, like many veterans in those years, I did all kinds of things while I was trying to figure out who I was and what I really wanted to do.

As I recall, going on television for the first time was a very strange experience — the lights were desperately hot and I wasn't sure that my demeanor or my face was right for the medium. The anonymity of radio was much more comfortable, but I realized that I was going to have to, somehow, make the switch if I was going to stay in the business.

One of my announcing jobs, and one of my funniest experiences back in those days, was on Mary Hartline's "Super Circus," broadcast live on Sundays on ABC-TV. The show had an audience made up mostly of children and it was done from the Civic Theater on Wacker Drive. They rehearsed between 1:00 and 4:00 in the afternoon, and then put it on the air at 5:00. One day, they had an elephant act with about ten young elephants, and we quickly learned that if you shined a light in the animals' eyes it opened up their bowels — involuntarily. Well, that's exactly what happened in rehearsal, and, suddenly, the stage was knee deep in elephant dung.

The rehearsal went on, and Mary Hartline, who was simply gorgeous, kept working while her legs, up to her knees, were spattered with elephant dung. So, with an hour to go before the audience was permitted in, the smell of elephant dung was still heavy in the hall — and there was a labor dispute as to who was going to clean up after the elephants! The stagehands insisted it wasn't their job, and everyone else said it wasn't their job. I remember there were a half a dozen of us who were wielding shovels, including the executive producer of the broadcast, Phil Patten, but not the stagehands. We finally got it cleaned up about 15 minutes before the 5:00 start time.

Well, the audience came rushing in, but since the smell was still heavy those poor kids who rushed to get a seat in the front row quickly changed their minds. Instead they began to back up toward the rear of the hall, and, naturally, that created a traffic jam of sorts.

Finally, the time came for us to go on the air, and about a half hour into the hour-long show, the elephants had to come out again. The staff figured the elephants had dumped it all, but they didn't realize that the elephants had some surprises for the audience. So, once again, the elephants unloaded. The cameramen, who were shooting the elephants as they went by, didn't want to focus on the backsides of the elephants, so they were shooting up above the stage. You've never seen anything so hilarious! But, even more challenging was the commercial that had to be done for Peter Pan peanut butter, the sponsor of the show. Luckily, the kid in the commercial was off-camera. I said, "Look at little Johnny as he spreads his Peter Pan peanut butter. Now he takes a

bite." Honest to God, as he took a bite of this sandwich there was a loop of saliva from the sandwich to his mouth, and as he took a look at it the kid started to cry — live on camera! All I can tell you is, it was the end of the sponsorship of Peter Pan peanut butter on "Super Circus!"

I left Chicago in 1951 because CBS made me an offer to come to New York, and the rest is history. But I can tell you that living in Chicago was an education since there were all kinds of fascinating things going on in radio and television there — from "Kukla, Fran and Ollie" to Dave Garroway to Studs Terkel. It was a great, "yeasty" place to be, and that's where I really tried to find out what the hell it was that I wanted to do. There was just a great vitality in radio and television in Chicago and you couldn't do anything "bad" because no one had ever done television before. I did so many different things in broadcasting in Chicago that it prepared me for everything to come.

Mike Wallace, member of television's Hall of Fame, has been a contributor to CBS-TV's "60 Minutes" for over 37 years.

Above: *Mike Wallace Rehearses in Chicago, c.1950*
Museum of Broadcast Communications Chicago

A Child's Best Friend | Ray Rayner

I was born in 1919 and grew up in New York City. When I first came to Chicago in 1953, I was a staff announcer at WBBM, where I did Standard Oil and other commercials for about a year. I remember we used to point our television camera to the east from the State-Lake Building. Well, one time the camera was focused on the Tribune Tower — it showed a women step out of the window and threaten to jump off the building. We called the police and told them about the situation, and I talked to the woman for about 25 minutes and kept her occupied long enough for them to grab her back in. So, I think that I helped save her life, and the story made the front pages of all the Chicago newspapers. I was described as CBS' new, young announcer — it was a very dramatic event.

In the fall of '53, I began my teenage dance show with Mina Kolb. Our first sponsor was Maybelline Cosmetics, and we used to begin the show with a close up of Mina's beautiful eyes. Mina was wonderful to work with and she was a wonderful actress. She and I would play records and we did the show for five years on Channel 2 from 1953 to 1958. It was on from 12:30 to 1:30 p.m. on Saturdays, and the teenagers would come in to the studio to dance. In those days, the boys all wore jackets and ties and the girls wore dresses. We had lots of recording stars come on our show because when they would tour the nation they would always stop in Chicago and spend the weekend in the city — people like Julius LaRosa.

At the same time, I also picked up a morning show where I would spin records like a radio disc jockey. I lasted on that show for a couple of years. Dave Garroway was our main competition on "The Today Show" in New York, so after about two years they decided to take my morning show off the air because we weren't doing anything in the ratings. Then, they asked me to do something else — a kid's show — but I didn't want to do that. They told me that I would lose the time slot altogether unless I made the change in format. So I agreed to do the show, and I agreed to wear a coverall-like jumpsuit they gave me. I stayed at CBS on that show from 1957 until 1961, when I was offered a job at WGN to do "The Dick Tracy Show." Then, in the fall of 1961, I played Sergeant Pettibone on WGN until, in 1962, I replaced Dick Coughlin as host of his morning show called "Breakfast With Bugs Bunny."

In 1964, the show was renamed "Ray Rayner and His Friends," and I stayed on that show for 19 years with my friends Cuddly Duddly and Chelveston the Duck. It was a very popular show and my ratings in Chicago beat "Today," "Good Morning America," and "The CBS Morning Show" combined — I had a 71% share! The WGN-TV studios were located on Bradley Place, and I always worked there while I was with WGN.

In the early days of "Ray Rayner and His Friends" I was still working on the other shows. Even in 1966, after the "Dick Tracy" show ended, I started another new kid's show called "Rocket to Adventure." I played the part of an astronaut, and that show lasted for about two seasons. So, I had "Ray Rayner and His Friends," "Bozo's Circus," and "Rocket to Adventure" all on the air each day — three shows a day for about six years. I would get up at about 5:45 in the morning, head down to the studio, and get there early to begin the preparations. Everything needed to be organized for me, and usually the cartoons and the gimmicks and the do-it-yourself projects were all set up. Of course, I would go to the Lincoln Park Zoo every few months and visit with Dr. Lester Fisher, a terrific guy and one of the most well-respected zoo directors in the world. Generally, I would tape about ten shows with him each visit and those shows would last me about ten weeks.

Ray Rayner served in the U.S. Army Air Force during WW II and spent two years in a German prison of war camp before attending Fordham University. Ray died on Jan. 21, 2004. His interview was not completed, but we felt it important to include his story because he affected so many lives during his long television career in Chicago.

A Conversation With Ms. Lee | Lee Phillip Bell

I was born in 1928 and grew up in Riverside, Illinois. My father had a flower shop in nearby Cicero, at 4904 W. Cermak Road, and I worked there from age four until college. My plan was to get into Northwestern University, but there were so many GI's coming back from the war that it was hard to get accepted. Eventually, I was admitted, and I graduated in 1950. I wanted to be a social worker, and I tried to get a job with the Cook County Welfare Department as a third class social worker. In the meantime, I went back to work for my dad at his flower shop.

About that time my older brother was asked to be on a WBKB-TV television program. A producer called our shop and said, "You have won an appearance on our morning television show." The appearance was free of charge — just a short segment on arranging flowers. So, my brother and I went down, and he did the arranging while I helped him. Well, when the show was over they asked my brother if he'd like to come back. We talked it over and agreed that I would come back. So, I planned a Hawaiian-themed show and brought tropical flowers and leis and arranged them. This time, I did it backwards, so that the public could see what I was doing. Most of the florists at the time did it facing them, so that the television viewer couldn't see a thing. The producers liked that I could do it backwards, and asked me back. So, I did more flower arranging appearances for about a year.

About that time, Lucky North, the only woman host who was doing shows at the time, was going to visit Japan for two weeks. She wanted a gal to take her place on her program, "The Lucky North Show," but didn't want Carmelita Pope or anybody who was really well known on television to do it — she didn't want to lose her job! When I was offered the opportunity I said, "I'd love to." So, I was all excited, but then the Cook County Welfare Department called me and asked me if I would take a job as a third class social worker. I said, "I'm awfully sorry, but I can't take it right now. But I will call you back in two weeks."

So, I did "The Lucky North Show" while she was away. I would get to the WBKB studio at 7:00 in the morning, and I'd sign on at 7:55 a.m. — with a prayer and a one minute public service announcement. I also had to announce the station schedule and read station breaks in between programs, like "The Gary Moore Show" and "The Art Linkletter Show." So, I really had to do everything! I recall doing an in-studio program with an automatic camera — no cameraman, just a camera pointed at you. It was a half-hour interview show, and one of the responsibilities was to arrange guests and ask them to come down to the studio. The interviewees included individuals who were promoting a motion picture or a prominent doctor — we would have doctors on from all the hospitals in the area. So, I got through the two weeks successfully when Lucky came back from her vacation and whispered to me, "Stick around kid, because I'm going to be leaving." She wanted to get married because she had met someone on her way to Japan.

While I was waiting around for Lucky to decide, Red Quinlan asked me if I would be a permanent member of the WBKB staff. I was just ecstatic! I did a program called "Shopping With Miss Lee,"which aired at 10:00 a.m. In 1956, CBS bought the station, and Frank Reynolds, Bruce Roberts, and I went over to their new station, while the rest of the staff stayed at WBKB.

I started doing "The Lee Phillip Show" right away, and it was in a large studio with three cameras — it was a big deal. At the same time, I was also doing the weather on the 10 p.m. news with Fahey Flynn and John Harrington doing the sports. On Saturdays, I also did a news show with Fahey and Jerry Dunphy in which I did feature segments on everything — from the Lincoln Park Zoo to all kinds of interesting stuff.

During those years I did interviews with many famous people who were coming through Chicago, and I traveled to other locations, including talking to Richard Nixon in Washington, D.C.. I had a wide range of people of my show, including many doctors, because my college major was related to medicine. I would also have many Hollywood movie stars on the show, like Marilyn Monroe, Bette Davis, John Wayne and Van Johnson, as well as musicians, like the Beatles. There weren't too many bad guests, and most of them were very good and interesting to talk to. I remember that Jerry Lewis was very difficult for men to interview. I told him when he came to Chicago that I had seen many of these difficult interviews. He asked me, "Oh, how did you like them?" I said, "Well, they scared me to death. I hope that you won't be that mean on my show." He said, "No, I'm pretty nice to women." As it turned out, he was very nice to me.

Lee Phillip Bell, with her husband, William Bell, created the popular CBS soap operas "The Bold and The Beautiful" and "The Young and The Restless."

'Chicago: The Last American City' | Mort Sahl

I met Hef' for the first time in 1954, when he and Victor Lownes were putting together *Playboy*. Hef' came to all the clubs, and I used to send him a champagne bucket full of Pepsi Cola — that was all he drank then, and no Jack Daniels with it. We would hang out, and he would always have the Saturday parties — he had a kind of Sunday salon. Hef never spared the "horses." He was, and is, a very high-style guy and the world's greatest host. When I got to Chicago it was famous for Adlai Stevenson, and when I left it was famous for Hugh Hefner. It was a transition period.

Mister Kelly's — they broke all the rules — it wasn't the Chez Paree yet, and it wasn't the Gate of Horn. It was a very hip club, and it had those bleachers up there so the couples could sit there. They used to serve coffee and donuts to those who were waiting in the snow for the next show in the good Chicago winter. Mister Kelly's had had only music acts, and I was the first guy to go in there and do comedy. It was wonderful in those years, and it was a very, very hip audience. We did long runs — once I did 31 weeks there. It just built and built because Chicago's got a core. It's not quite New York and not Los Angeles — it has a core. People would bring other people back. It was exciting and we would go all night.

I lived at 25 E. Delaware, and, then, later on, Hef put the house together. At that time, he was living near Ohio Street where they put out *Popular Mechanics*. He had an apartment over there with suntan lamps over his bed and drawers for his shirts and socks that went one way to the bathroom and the other way into his bedroom. He used to work all day, and then I would meet him around 2 a.m. and we would go prowl. We would go to the Cloister in the Maryland Hotel. Hef' was a very dapper dude, and full of intellectual curiosity.

Of course, Chicago was humming then. All the advertising men with Leo Burnett were on North Michigan Avenue, and Adlai Stevenson was brewing up there on the Gold Coast.

I knew Larry Fanning down at the *Sun-Times* and Abe Marowitz up there on the bench and Herman Kogan, who was then the book editor at the *Sun-Times*. I knew Herman Kogan very well. Herman introduced me to Leonard Kauffman, who wrote "Bad Day at Black Rock." During my years in Chicago, there were so many famous people in the newspaper corps — there were four newspapers back then.

It was a jumping community, with the gang down at University of Chicago and up at Northwestern — I mean there were a lot of ideas floating around town. We worked very well with the college kids. Chicago was very organic, and you could get a conversation anywhere.

Later on, Hef got the house on State Street. I was the first person to stay there, and I was the first celebrity to write an article for *Playboy*. Everything was beginning to really brew then because we were on our way to the Kennedy convention in Los Angeles. Chicago really was the "first city," and not the "second city." It jumped all night and Hef' and I used to go to Musket and Henriksen drugstore that was open 24 hours. Finally, when he put in the club down there on Oak Street, everybody used to come by and get that steak sandwich with cheese at 5 o'clock in the morning. It went all night, and the Bunnies stayed at the house and they used to go out and ride their horses in Grant Park in the morning at sunrise. There was something going on all night. It was really a wild time. Then, Kup started his television show and gave us an awful lot of help there.

When Hef' moved into his house on State Street, I brought Frank Sinatra there at his request — and I brought Bob Hope over at his request. We had a lot of good times, and Hef' was staying up all night writing his "Playboy Philosophy," and he would be up four days at a time typing the column. Chicago was percolating. I knew Studs and I knew Garroway and Mike Royko and Dan Sorkin on the radio. We would stay up all night and then go over to the radio station and heckle Sorkin when he was on the air.

When I started performing in Chicago I did those good, long engagements where I would get up and do my stuff about the Republicans. During the 1950s I had plenty of stuff to do about the Republicans, and Jake Arvey was running Stevenson's campaign. I think that Adlai Stevenson was the finest man whom I ever met, and his son was a pretty great senator, too.

Chicago was anything but the "second city." It was the last American city, and it was with a lot of gusto. Everyone was "deep" in the community, and you could do a lot of community jokes. I didn't do a general act. I did stuff about the town. It was really popping in Chicago in those days, and every time they opened another neighborhood further north, I predicted disaster and it was always bountiful. My memories of those years are wonderful. Hef' said to me the other day, "You know, it's not nostalgia. We knew it was great then."

Mort Sahl was born in Montreal and grew up in Los Angeles. He still performs in his trademark sweater with newspaper in hand.

Mort Sahl, c.1958
Playboy Archive

Taking Chances | Hugh Hefner

In January of 1953, I was working as circulation manager for a children's magazine called *Children's Activities*. I was being paid well, but I also felt trapped and frustrated — it seemed that my life was going nowhere. Just a month before that, in December, I attended a Steinmetz High School reunion. My best buddy from high school, Jim Brophy, hosted and wrote the stage show there, a kind of variety show that included some comedy acts and songs. That experience reminded me of how I felt in high school, which was a very creative time for me. I wrote plays and songs, drew cartoons, and worked on the school paper. At that time in my life, I had hoped that my adult life would be like that, too. Instead, I think I felt very much like an outsider. I felt that all my dreams and aspirations from high school and earlier had been forced aside.

When I went back to do that show, it just reignited those yearnings. I remember standing on the Michigan Avenue bridge over the river in January, feeling really lost, and wondering if I was turning into my parents. It was in the weeks and months that immediately followed that I started making plans for *Playboy*. While I worked at *Children's Activities* during the day, I worked on *Playboy* at night. The notion of starting *Playboy*, of course, was impossible, because I didn't have any money. I literally had nothing, but I just did it. I managed to borrow some money from a local loan company and a bank as domestic loans — putting my furniture up as collateral. Then, I formed a corporation and got friends and relatives and anybody to invest a total of $8,000. Of course, you can't really start a magazine for that kind of money, but through a local printer I made a deal where I could pay half of the printing bill in 30 days and the other half in 60 days. The gap between the printing and the money coming in is what financed the company, and I printed 70,000 copies of the first issue of *Playboy*.

The original notion was that I needed some kind of gimmick for that first issue. Well, 3-D comics and movies were very popular at the time, such as "The House of Wax." So, I thought about doing a 3-D nude pictorial, and we actually photographed it. Then, I discovered that putting those little green and red glasses in each issue would be too expensive, because I really didn't have any money. At that same time, I discovered that the Marilyn Monroe calendar that everybody had heard about, but nobody had seen, was owned by the John Baumgarth Calendar Company on North Avenue — not too far from where I had grown up. So, I drove out there in my beat up '41 Chevy. John Baumgarth was there — he was a shirtsleeve kind of guy — and I had my best day. I think he just saw in me a kind of entrepreneurial guy like himself, and he gave me the rights to reproduce the Marilyn Monroe calendar picture for $500 — and he threw in the color separations. The separations alone would have cost me over $1,000. So, Marilyn was the first *Playboy* playmate.

I originally wasn't going to call the magazine *Playboy*. I was going to call the it Stag Party, inspired by a book called *The Stag at Eve*, which was filled with *New Yorker*-type cartoons, only sexier. In November of 1953, however, I got a cease and desist order from the lawyer of a men's magazine called *Stag*. Since I already had some second thoughts about the title, I changed the name to *Playboy*, and changed the stag symbol that I was going to use into a rabbit in a tuxedo. The rest, as they say, is history.

The audience for the magazine was bachelors — young, single guys — there had never been a magazine like that before. *Esquire* had been for the older guys, and *Esquire* itself, after the war, had already changed, taking the cartoons and pin-up pictures out. The successful men's magazines after the war were actually outdoor adventure magazines like *True*, *Argosy*, and *Stag*. *True* had a circulation of about 2,500,000 copies at that point. However, I had no competition for the kind of magazine that *Playboy* was.

We didn't have centerfolds in the early issues of the magazine. In fact, the playmates in the first year were actually calendar pictures from Baumgarth. Then, once we were able to start shooting them ourselves in the second year, that's where the girl-next-door concept came from. Both locally and nationally, *Playboy* became a "hot" magazine very quickly. We started the magazine with a print run of 70,000 copies, and by 1960, we were selling over 1,000,000 copies an issue.

About that time, I started to branch out into a number of different areas, and all of these events completely changed my life. I reinvented myself, and came out from behind my desk. First, I started hosting a syndicated television show called "Playboy's Penthouse," which was a "conceptual" party in what appeared to be my penthouse apartment. We taped the show at WBKB-TV, Channel 7 — "Red" Quinlan's station on State Street, next to the State-Lake Theater. Next, in February 1960, the very first Playboy Club opened on Walton Street, just west of Michigan Avenue, and was hugely successful. Now, we ran into a problem with the City of Chicago because they refused to give us a liquor license. The city suddenly decided that the key clubs were illegal. Well, there had been key clubs in Chicago since the 1920s, including the Key Club and the Gaslight Club — which was one of the inspirations for the Playboy Club. But, because we were Playboy, they refused to give us a license. We took them to court and beat them.

One of the first problems we had with the city was over the Playboy Jazz Festival, held in the summer of 1959. Initially, we were going to hold the festival in combination with the city and the Pan American Games. The event was all planned, and we even held a press conference with a representative from Mayor Daley's Office announcing the event. But then the Mayor's Office got "heat" from the Archdiocese of Chicago. In those days, of course, Chicago was a very Catholic city, and the cardinal had a heavy hand in the politics of the time. The Chicago Archdiocese, historically, was also responsible for the "production code" in Hollywood, as well as the League of Decency. So, I was very much aware of their activity in terms of sexual behavior. That pressure got the city to pull out of its association with Playboy. So, we turned around and put on the jazz festival ourselves at the Chicago Stadium. There was a lot of publicity surrounding that decision, and we got a lot of sympathetic press because of the decision by Mayor Daley to turn on us.

The festival was wonderful, with three days and two nights of different jazz musicians. It was the greatest jazz event ever held in terms of the stars that appeared. Everybody was there: Louis Armstrong, Ella Fitzgerald, Sarah Vaughn, the Count Basie Orchestra, the Duke Ellington Orchestra, the Stan Kenton Orchestra, Miles Davis' group, Dizzy Gillespie's group, Dave Brubeck with Paul Desmond, Cannonball Adderley's group, the Hi-Lo's, June Christie — nobody had ever put so many artists together in one event. All of this happened because jazz was the music I grew up with in Chicago.

In the early 1960s, it was a time of tremendous growth and success for us. But, as you can see, it wasn't without its problems. It was in December of 1962 that they arrested Lenny Bruce for obscenity at the Gate of Horn. We were already good friends, and I arranged for Lenny to use our lawyer, Morrie Rosenfield. That same month I started writing an editorial series called "The Playboy Philosophy," in which I addressed these issues concerning the Chicago police, the Catholic connection and what they did to Lenny. In June of 1963, the police came and arrested me, and the FBI continued to collect information about me, although I wasn't aware of all of it. In fact, we had the first visit from the FBI in 1955, and I recently learned that J. Edgar Hoover had assigned a guy to read every line of *Playboy*.

I was a very liberal kid growing up, and I had strong feelings about the civil rights movement throughout the 1950s and '60s. Back in those days, black musicians and singers could appear in white clubs, but not comics. The first black comic to work in a club that was white was Dick Gregory, and we hired him. He worked out of the South Side in some of the black clubs, but was doing so poorly that he was actually working part time in a garage — and thinking about quitting. He came to work at the Playboy Club in Chicago, and at that point we had clubs in several other cities, including New Orleans, Miami and New York City. What developed was almost like a vaudeville circuit, because we had our own network of clubs. Eventually, we had about 20 clubs around the country, and the entertainers would go from one club to another and could actually work a whole year just doing Playboy Clubs. Dick Gregory was a huge success, and *Time* magazine did a big story about him after he worked at the Playboy Club. All of this led to the breaking of the color barrier for black comedians, and is something I'm very proud to have been a part of.

Hef's World

On the Set of "Playboy's Penthouse," 1959
Playboy Archive

At Work, c.1958

Sammy Davis Jr. on "Playboy's Penthouse," 1959

Above and right: *The Playboy Mansion, 1340 N. State Parkway, c.1959*

ACKNOWLEDGEMENTS

The interviews that comprise this book were conducted over a 15 month period beginning in the summer of 2003. We thank those who took time from their busy schedules to talk to us, and sincerely regret not being able to include each person we spoke to. Without the contributions of all our interviewees, this book would not have been possible. They include, in alphabetical order: Robert Adamowski, Leonard Amari, Bruce Bachmann, Michael Bakalis, Kent Beauchamp, Lee Phillip Bell, Maury Berman, Shelley Berman, Trudy Bers, Phil Bouzeos, Eric Bronsky, Jim Brosnan U.S. Senator Hillary Rodham Clinton (D-NY), Bob Dauber, Raymond DeGroote, Hugh Downs, Richard Duchossois, Bruce DuMont, Harriet Wilson Ellis, Judge Richard Elrod, Jerry Field, Georgie Anne Geyer, Bill Gleason, Al Hall, Milo Hamilton, Hugh Hefner, Bob Herguth, Tom Hilliard, Katie Hogan, Richard Jaffee, Steve Jajkowski, Michael James, Bill Jauss, Mary Robinson Kalista, U.S. District Judge Charles Kocoras, Morton Kondrake, Margie Korshak, Joe Levinson, Ramsey Lewis, Richard Lang, Erin McCann, Illinois Supreme Court Justice Mary Ann McMorrow, Richard Melman, Norman Mark, Johnny Morris, Mike Nussbaum, James O'Connor, Gene Oliver, Jim Parker, Sheldon Patinkin, Bruno Pasquinelli, Tony Pasquinelli, Jerry Petacque, Billy Pierce, Bob Polster, Mike Pyle, Ward Quall, Sterling "Red" Quinlan, Ray Rayner, Jack Rosenberg, Ronnie Rubenstein, Mort Sahl, Carmen Salvino, Rich Samuels, Warner Saunders, Chuck Schaden, Richard Skinner, Wyonella Smith, Don Stonesifer, William Thayer, Ferdy Thillens, Mel Thillens, Jr., Honorable James R. Thompson, Ruth Marion Tobias, Jane Upin, Mary Frances Veeck, Mike Wallace, Clark Weber, Jeff Wien, Joel Weisman, Honorable Jesse White, Sheila Morris Williams, Harvey Wittenberg, Bruce Wolf, Edward Yalowitz, Joel Zimberoff and Steve Zucker.

A second group of individuals were both interviewees and referrals to other people interviewed in this book. They include: Bruce Bachmann, Bruce DuMont, Richard Melman, James O'Connor, Jack Rosenberg, Warner Saunders, Don Stonesifer and Bruce Wolf. Thanks to Amy Bonitatibus, Deputy Press Secretary for Sen. Clinton, for coordinating her interview.

We also thank Richard Cahan for his invaluable advice as an editor, designer and photo editor. His boundless enthusiasm and love of books helped, too.

ABOUT THE PHOTOS

The photographs in this book are drawn from a variety of sources, including public and corporate collections as well as individual lenders. Photo credits appear underneath the picture's caption. All uncredited photos are from the collection of Michael Williams. We thank everyone who contributed photographs to this book, especially those who opened their personal archives. Lee Phillip Bell, Eric Bronsky, Hugh Downs, Hugh Hefner, Robert Middaugh, Billy Pierce, Jack Rosenberg and Bill Swislow all provided images from their own collections, most never before published.

The wonderful photos from the *Chicago Sun-Times* come through the assistance of Ron Theel, Herb Ballard, Trina Higgins and Dan Miller. The *Sun-Times* archive is simply the best in the city, and we strongly encourage all authors and researchers to begin their searches there. Copies of *Sun-Times* credited photos can be purchased from the paper by calling 312-321-3000 or emailing pubinfo@suntimes.com.

Thanks also go to Julia Bachrach and Robert Middaugh of the Chicago Park District, Jeff Stern and Bruce Moffat of the Chicago Transit Authority, Teri Thomerson of *Playboy* magazine and the staff of the Harold Washington Branch of the Chicago Public Library.

When available, the photographer's name has been included with their photo. Unfortunately, there are many instances where this credit could not be provided, due to lack of, or unreliable, captioning. Any information about these photographers would be greatly appreciated, and we encourage readers to contact us at realchicago@rcn.com.

SUBJECT INDEX

Edited by Michael Williams and Neal Samors.
Produced by Michael Williams.
Book designed by Michael Williams.

Printed in Canada by Friesens Corporation.

ISBN: 0-9725456-4-6 (Case)

Front Cover: *Chicago River on a Foggy Day, 1955* (Photograph by Bill Sturm *Chicago Sun-Times*)
Frontispiece: *Chicago, 1957*

For more information on this book as well as the authors' other works visit our website: realchicago.net
E-mail: realchicago@rcn.com